When Pastors *Prey*

When Pastors *Prey*

Overcoming Clergy Sexual Abuse of Women

Edited by Valli Boobal Batchelor

WHEN PASTORS PREY
Overcoming Clergy Sexual Abuse of Women
Edited by Valli Boobal Batchelor

WCC Publications is the book publishing programme of the World Council of Churches. Founded in 1948, the WCC promotes Christian unity in faith, witness and service for a just and peaceful world. A global fellowship, the WCC brings together more than 349 Protestant, Orthodox, Anglican and other churches representing more than 560 million Christians in 110 countries and works cooperatively with the Roman Catholic Church. Opinions expressed in this volume are those of the authors.

Cover design: Josh Messner
Book design and typesetting: Josh Messner
ISBN: 978-2-8254-1566-5

World Council of Churches
150 route de Ferney, P.O. Box 2100
1211 Geneva 2, Switzerland
http://publications.oikoumene.org

Contents

Part One. Identifying the Problem

Part Two. The Experience of Abuse

Part Three. Churches Addressing Clergy Misconduct

Part Four. Stopping Abuse for Good

Prologue

The Global Scourge of Violence against Women

Jimmy Carter

I am pleased to address the vital role of religion in providing a foundation for—or correcting—the global scourge of discrimination and violence against women. As will be seen, my remarks represent the personal views of a Christian layman and a former political leader.

There are international agreements as well as our own Holy Scriptures that guide us: Article 2 of the Universal Declaration of Human Rights states: "Everyone is entitled to all the rights and freedoms set forth in this Declaration, without distinction of any kind, such as race, color, sex, language, religion, political or other opinion, origin...or other status." The Holy Bible tells us that "There is neither Jew nor Greek, there is neither bond nor free, there is neither male nor female: for ye are all one in Christ Jesus" (Galatians 3:28). Every generic religious text encourages believers to respect essential human dignity, yet some selected scriptures are interpreted to justify the derogation or inferiority of women and girls, our fellow human beings. All of us have a responsibility to acknowledge and address the gross acts of discrimination and violence against women that occur every day. Here are some well-known examples:

Globally, at least one in three women and girls is beaten or sexually abused in her lifetime. (U.N. Commission on the Status of Women, February, 2000).

Our Carter Center has been deeply involved in the Republic of Congo. In war zones where order has broken down, horrific and sometimes lethal rape has become a tactic of warfare practiced by all sides.

In a study in 2000, the U.N. estimated that at least 60 million girls who should be alive are "missing" from various populations, mostly in Asia, as a result of sex-selective abortions, infanticide or neglect.

According to UNICEF, an estimated one million children, mostly girls, enter the sex trade each year, and the U.N. estimates that 4 million women and girls are trafficked annually.

In some Islamic nations, women are restricted in their movements, punished for permitting the exposure of an arm or ankle, deprived of education, prohibited from driving a car or competing with men for a job. If a woman is raped, she is often most severely punished as the guilty party in the crime. The same discriminatory thinking lies behind the continuing gender gap in pay and explains why so few women hold political office, even in most Western democracies.

You are all familiar with these facts, and I know you are considering the causes and possible solutions to this serious global problem. There are clear indications that progress is being made in the secular world. We have seen women chosen as leaders in nations as diverse as India, Pakistan, Indonesia, Israel, Great Britain, Ireland, Chile, Germany, the Philippines, and Nicaragua. Their support came from citizens who are predominantly Hindu, Islamic, Jewish, and Christian, and include two of the three largest democracies on earth.

It is ironic that women are now welcomed into all major professions and other positions of authority, but are branded as inferior and deprived of the equal right to serve God in positions of religious leadership. The plight of abused women is made more acceptable by the mandated subservience of women by religious leaders.

Most Bible scholars acknowledge that the Holy Scriptures were written when male dominance prevailed in every aspect of life. Men could have multiple sex partners (King Solomon had 300 wives and 700 concubines), but adulterous behavior by a woman could be punished by stoning to death—then, in the time of Christ and, in some societies, 2000 years later.

I realize that devout Christians can find adequate scripture to justify either side in this debate, but there is one incontrovertible fact concerning the relationship between Jesus Christ and women: he never condoned sexual discrimination or the implied subservience of women. The exaltation and later reverence for Mary, as Jesus' mother, is an even more vivid indication of the special status of women in Christian theology.

I have taught Bible lessons for more than 65 years, and I know that Paul forbade women to worship with their heads covered, to braid their hair, or to wear rings, jewelry, or expensive clothes. It is obvious to most modern day Christians that Paul was not mandating permanent or generic theological policies. In a letter to Timothy, Paul also expresses a prohibition against women's teaching men, but we know—and he knew—that Timothy himself was instructed by his mother and grandmother.

At the same time, in Paul's letter to the Romans, he listed and thanked twenty-eight outstanding leaders of the early churches, at least ten of whom were women. "I commend to you our sister Phoebe, a deacon of the church…greet Prisca and Aquila, who work with me in Christ Jesus…greet Mary, who has worked very hard among you…greet Andronicus and Junia, my relatives who were in prison with me; they are prominent among the apostles, and they were in Christ before I was…greet Philologus, Julia, Nereus and his sister, and Olympas, and all the saints who are with them."

It is clear that during the early Christian era women served as deacons, priests, bishops, apostles, teachers, and prophets. It wasn't until the fourth century that dominant Christian leaders, all men, twisted and distorted Holy Scriptures to perpetuate their ascendant positions within the religious hierarchy.

My own Southern Baptist Convention leaders ordained in recent years that women must be "subservient" to their husbands and prohibited from serving as deacons, pastors, chaplains in the military service, or teachers of men. They based this on a few carefully selected quotations from Saint Paul and also Genesis, claiming that Eve was created second to Adam and was responsible for original sin. This was in conflict with my belief that we are all equal in the eyes of God. The Roman Catholic Church and many others revere the Virgin Mary but consider women unqualified to serve as priests.

This view that the Almighty considers women to be inferior to men is not restricted to one religion or tradition. Its influence does not stop at the walls of the church, mosque, synagogue, or temple. Women are prevented from playing a full and equal role in many faiths, creating an environment in which violations against women are justified.

The truth is that male religious leaders have had—and still have—an option to interpret holy teachings either to exalt or subjugate women. They have, for their own selfish ends, overwhelmingly chosen the latter. Their continuing choice provides the foundation or justification for much of the pervasive persecution and abuse of women throughout the world. This is in clear violation not just of the Universal Declaration of Human Rights but also the teachings of Jesus Christ, the Apostle Paul, Moses and the prophets, Muhammad, and founders of other great religions—all of whom have called for proper and equitable treatment of all the children of God. It is time we had the courage to challenge these views and set a new course that demands equal rights for women and men, girls and boys.

At their most repugnant, the belief that women are inferior human beings in the eyes of God gives excuses to the brutal husband who beats his wife, the soldier who rapes a woman, the employer who has a lower pay scale for women employees, or parents who decide to abort a female embryo. It also costs many millions of girls and women control over their own bodies and lives, and continues to deny them fair and equal access to education, health care, employment, and influence within their own communities.

Recently, I presented my concerns to a group of fellow leaders known as The Elders, who represent practicing Protestants, Catholics, Muslims, and Hindus. We are no longer active in politics and are free to express our honest opinions. We decided to draw particular attention to the role of religious and traditional leaders in obstructing the campaign for equality and human rights, and promulgated a statement that declares: "The justification of discrimination against women and girls on grounds of religion or tradition, as if it were prescribed by a Higher Authority, is unacceptable."

Having served as local, state, national, and world leaders, we understand why many public officials can be reluctant to question ancient religious and traditional premises—an arena of great power and sensitivity. Despite this, we are calling on all those with influence to challenge and change the harmful teachings and practices—in religious and secular life—that justify discrimination against women and to acknowledge and emphasize the positive messages of equality and human dignity.

Jimmy Carter
Former U.S. President

Preface

CHRISTINE HOUSEL AND FULATA LUSUNGU MOYO

In giving attention to clergy sexual abuse of vulnerable adult women, we want to raise awareness about a problem silenced for far too long. We hope to transform cultural perceptions that condone violence against women. And we challenge churches to truly become "safe havens" for women. No clergy abuse of power, exploitation, or rape should be masked by the erroneous term "affair."

This project is a joint initiative of the World Student Christian Federation (WSCF) and the World Council of Churches (WCC), building on the work on gender that each of these sister international ecumenical organizations have undertaken over the last several decades.

The WSCF is a global federation of over one hundred affiliated student Christian national movements which span the world. It is a hope-giving voice for the current generation and for generations to come.

Publication of this volume is also supported by the World Council of Churches (WCC), specifically by its Programme on Women in Church and Society. The WCC is a worldwide fellowship of 345 churches seeking unity, a common witness for justice and peace and Christian service that enhances dignity for all. Both the WSCF and the WCC have provided leadership in calling the church to examine itself and its own practices regarding the full inclusion of both women and men and empowering women and men to partner together in addressing gender, and all other, injustices.

To illuminate clergy exploitation of women, we have brought abused women's experiences together with the voices of experts who have been influential in understanding this problem and designing real strategies for eliminating it altogether.

It is deeply ironic that while ecumenical Christianity has advocated and labored for social justice and gender equality in society and its institutions for more than sixty years, Christian churches themselves remain a deep source of and abiding locus of gender injustice. Nowhere is this more graphically and painfully exhibited than in clergy sexual abuse.

This abuse happens frequently in many different church communities but is rarely dealt with adequately in any. Experts estimate that 90–95 percent of victims of clergy sexual exploitation are women of varied ages who are unable to see themselves as victims and are often trapped in a combination of confusion, guilt, shame and self-blame. Women victims who remain silenced by religious leaders suffer severe consequences, from loss of dignity to depression to suicide.

How can we prevent sexual abuse by religious leaders? Breaking the cycle of silence is a crucial element of prevention, Naming it correctly as an abuse of power is another. Understanding and evaluating the Christian tradition's long ambivalence toward and unjust treatment of women is also key. This book aims to unfold the dynamics of sexual abuse by those who purport to be caregivers, to listen to the stories of those who have suffered clergy abuse, to lay bare its cultural and religious roots, and to present practices and policies that can be used to combat such exploitation worldwide. We sincerely hope that you will find it helpful in your quest for understanding the hurt and damage caused by clergy sexual misconduct, for devising sensitive pastoral care, for engendering personal and ecclesial healing, and for pursuing systemic justice.

Christine Housel   *Fulata Lusungu Moyo*
General Secretary   Programme Executive
World Student Christian Federation   Women in Church and Society
                                             World Council of Churches

Editor's Introduction

Valli Boobal Batchelor

This prophetic project breaks a longstanding silence about a problem that undermines the very foundations of pastoral work and institutional Christianity: sexual abuse of women by clergy.

An outcome of more than six years of experience with adult women survivors of clergy sexual abuse from Asia Pacific, North America, Europe, Africa, Latin America and the Caribbean, the volume gathers multiple resources and insights to address the problem.

Clergy sexual abuse of children has received global media and public attention and has resulted in many changes that will protect children in churches. Yet little has been written about the more widespread and just as devastating phenomenon of abuse of adult women by clergy—a silent killer within Christian churches around the world.

According to Columbia Theological Seminary's Pamela Cooper-White, 90 to 95 percent of victims of clergy sexual misconduct are female congregants. These victims are often so trapped in confusion, guilt, shame and self-blame that they are unable to see themselves as victims. Clinical research from the FaithTrust Institute indicates that women victims are likely to remain silent, with many suffering severe consequences that range from depression to suicide.

Dr Randel Everett, Executive Director and CEO of the Baptist General Convention of Texas, acknowledges that such abuse causes a chain-reaction of damage to multiple victims, "first the victim herself, then her whole family system, and eventually the congregation and the community." Yet very few church organizations or religious institutions have begun breaking down the taboos surrounding clergy sexual abuse of women. As church communities across the English-speaking world are being torn apart by disclosures of sexual abuse by well-respected leaders, the churches have repeatedly shown their inability to respond adequately to the pain of survivors. The covering-up of this shame by church hierarchies continues to cost churches financial strain and bankruptcies, quite apart from deeply undermining the faith of the people.

Editing this book project has been a challenging experience, a real exposure to the inhuman manner in which churches typically respond to those who come forward with disclosures of clergy sexual abuse. It has taken courage, perseverance, strength and stamina—from me and from many of my collaborators and the contributors—to pursue this project.

Here credit must be given above all to the survivors and supporters around the world who have dared to share their painful accounts of clergy sexual abuse. They have courageously taken a collective stand against this violence and are breaking the long silence that only serves to further oppress and exploit women in churches. Drawing from their courage, we were further inspired to do our part for transformation to take place.

A further reason for this publication is the failure of churches to address the root issue of power imbalance between clergy and sexually abused adult parishioners. Almost every contribution to this book raises the issue of *power*. Yet disclosures of sexual abuse between adults are easily dismissed or down-played as "consensual affairs," without considering the real issues—the abuse of power, the clergy's violations of the sacred trust of ministries, the breach of fiduciary responsibility and the violation of professional boundaries.

Like other helping professionals, clergy have a stream of people seeking their aid on intimate matters. In addition to the power which arises in parallel secular situations, however, is the religious significance of clergy—who have access to the deepest fears, longings and pain of their congregants. They are seen as God's representatives on earth and carry an extraordinary amount of trust and power. All clergy and those who work in professional relationships of trust need to recognize their grave responsibility to all those in their care and to acknowledge that, across genders, such intimacy may translate into sexual attraction and arousal. When that happens, the clergy person is under the strongest prohibition, since to cross the bounds of propriety is to undermine the psychological underpinning of the entire ministerial relationship. Clergy sexual abuse of women needs to be seen as a gross violation of the power of a minister towards his parishioner. There should be no confusion of clergy sexual abuse of women with or acceptance of it as a consensual affair between adults. In this relationship, there are *no* equals, and the responsibility rests squarely with the clergy person, who needs to be held to account. The tendency to blame the woman needs to be resisted and not institutionalized.

This book is also a contribution toward opening honest and difficult dialogues between survivor groups and churches. At a time when the churches have become more self-critical because of revelations and acknowledgment of abuse, there is a window of opportunity to address this widespread but almost hidden shame in a way that rebuilds rather than destroys the institutions of the church and its professing ministry. By recognizing that the problem is no longer confined to the occasional "rogue pastor" but is a serious, even systemic, issue, churches and their governing bodies, both ordained and lay, can be equipped to address the issues and the vulnerabilities of their organizations. This project gives voice especially to the experiences of adult women abused by clergy—as theirs is the voice that must be heard first and with respect.

We realize that some may be surprised and may even be angered by this publication and judge it to be unfair and detrimental to the good works of churches. Since clergy sexual abuse of women is contrary to a right understanding of Christian faith and its biblical mandate, it may seem wrong to suggest that abuse, avoidance of accountability and obfuscation are the norm in churches. There is always the concern that revelations of such a dark side of Christian churches may leave a misleading picture of church communities and their leaders. Yet as revealed in this book, instances of clergy sexual abuse of women may be far more than what many of us have realized, and certain biblical interpretations continue to be used by church leaders to justify the oppression and subjugation of women in churches.

Church leaders can be very articulate when speaking about the Christian message of love, forgiveness, healing, justice and mercy. Yet in the area of sexual abuse by its clergy, church leaders frequently get caught up in protecting the perpetrator and the institution and engaging in behavior that further harms the victims. Demands for justice by those who have suffered at the hands of clergy are frequently undermined by the legal and financial concerns of the institution and the desire to protect the church from scandal.

While churches have begun developing public policies and procedures to adequately respond to disclosures of abuse, their present and past failures are a sign of how far many of them are from understanding the issue of clergy sexual abuse—especially when the victim is an adult woman. Even the best policies and procedures will be undermined, unless the underlying attitudes of those who administer and are bound by them are changed.

The painful survivor stories, and the accounts of indifference, hostility and obstruction by church hierarchies toward the women involved are unpleasant and disturbing, but we believe that it is healthy and necessary to bring these church realities to the surface. Although the analysis presented in this book deals with clergy abuse of adult women, it does not minimize the situation of sexual abuse of children and men by clergy or its horrific consequences. The focus of this book is on the protection of women and the prevention of abuse by clergy across all cultures. Unless churches model and practice respect for women, how can they be effective role models for equality and peace in the world?

The Book

With a prologue by Jimmy Carter, *When Pastors Prey* not only brings forward the stories of many women whose trust has been abused by their pastors, it also offers a helpful framework in which to understand and address the problem, in four parts:

> Part 1. Identifying the Problem
> Part 2. The Experience of Abuse
> Part 3. Churches Addressing Clergy Misconduct
> Part 4. Stopping Abuse for Good
> Additional Resources

Ultimately, clergy sexual abuse of women is one of the most horrific expressions of longstanding Christian misunderstanding and mistreatment of women. This volume illuminates not only the phenomenon but its roots and—in brave hope—its cures.

The World Student Christian Federation (WSCF) and the World Council of Churches (WCC) have jointly played a role of historic significance by pooling together the knowledge, experiences and voices of pioneering researchers, experts, survivors, advocates, theologians, legal and health specialists, and relevant organizations to create a book that we hope will begin a cultural transformation within Christian churches worldwide.

WSCF—a radical, hope-giving voice of current and future generations—is independent enough from religious institutions. Hence it has a unique capacity to be the leader for change, and it builds on its work through more than 100 affiliated student Christian movements spanning six regions. The WCC serves as an unparalleled leader for justice and peace to influence worldwide churches. Beyond these two sponsoring organizations, the International Association of Women Judges (IAWJ) adds a global justice dimension to the issue with the advocacy for legal sanctions against "sextortion"—a newly introduced legal campaign to criminalize sexual abuse of women by those in positions of power. Likewise the World Health Organisation (WHO) highlights the prevention of such sexual abuse as a global health issue of priority.

We hope to make this publication available far and wide and to offer related seminars in various regions to further disseminate the message—a vision that will be possible through continuing support and collaborative partnerships with churches and secular communities. Above all, we hope that this book and its insights and resources will reach the following groups:

First, we hope this book reaches Christian seminaries and is read by those involved in training clergy *and* the clergy whom they train. The training of future clergy on the issue of sexual abuse of women will be instrumental in shifting the attitudes which lie at the heart of the abuse. Clergy need to be clearly aware that they are persons of power and trust, and the misuse of that power is central to the problem of sexual abuse.

Second, we hope that this book will be read by those responsible for the development of church policies and procedures. Undoubtedly this will not be a comfortable or comforting book to read. Yet this kind of discomfort needs to be faced, in order adequately to respond to disclosures of such abuse.

Third, we hope this book will be read by those who counsel women who are or have been sexually abused by clergy or other professionals in a relationship of trust. Counselors need to be aware that, though there are parallels with different forms of abuse, there are some dimensions which belong distinctively to abuse of adult women.

Lastly, but not of least importance, we hope that this book will be read by survivors. As a validation of these women's life experiences, this book names the truth of the reality facing adult victims of clergy abuse and points out that real responsibility lies with the clergy and the church. This book is needed as an encouragement to victims and survivors to be open to their own truth, to seek support and healing and to claim life in all its fullness again. We also hope that they are empowered with an understanding of what to expect from the churches if they choose to seek justice.

As editor, my heartfelt hopes lie with the churches, congregations and secular organizations who feel challenged to change their attitudes and actions when they confront the reality of sexual abuse of women in the churches and take their first tentative steps toward making all churches around the world safer for women.

Contributors

Rev. Nicqi Ashwood is an ordained minister with the United Church in Jamaica and the Cayman Islands. She currently serves as the Education in Mission Secretary for the Caribbean and North America Council for Mission (CANACOM). She has collaborated with the Women's Desks of the World Communion of Reformed Churches (WCRC) and the World Council of Churches (WCC) in workshop presentations promoting awareness and advocacy for abused women. She contributed articles for the regional Women's Bible Studies Manual.

Dr. Valli Boobal Batchelor is an educator, an intercultural artist and an advocate for gender justice and peace. She co-founded Journey towards Hope Projects in Malaysia with her husband, Dr. Andrew Batchelor. To date the projects received awards for tapping the vast potential of culture and the arts to engage, educate and empower participants and promote messages of violence prevention in Asia Pacific, Middle East, Europe and North America. She is a World Council of Churches' Mover of Just Peace and an expert delegate to UN Commission on Status of Women. She holds a doctorate in banking and finance.

Rev. Dr. Garlinda Burton is the General Secretary of the General Commission on the Status and Role of Women of the United Methodist Church. She is a specialist in racial and gender issues in the media, academia, church and corporate life, and she frequently conducts training on combating sexism, classism and racism for media professionals, educators, businesses and church leaders.

President Jimmy Carter was United States president from 1977–81, and was awarded the 2002 Nobel Peace Prize. This prologue is derived from a presentation he prepared for the Elders, an independent group of eminent global leaders, brought together by Nelson Mandela, who offer their influence and experience to support peace building, help address major causes of human suffering and promote the shared interests of humanity. The speech was delivered to the Parliament of the World Religions in 2009 and is used here by permission.

Rev. Dr. Pamela Cooper-White is Professor of Pastoral Theology, Care and Counseling at Columbia Theological Seminary, and Co-Director of the Atlanta Theological Association's program in Pastoral Counseling. She holds doctorates from Harvard University and the Institute for Clinical Social Work, Chicago. In 2005, she received the American Association of Pastoral Counselors' national award for "Distinguished Achievement in Research and Writing" She is the author of *The Cry of Tamar: Violence against Women and the Church's Response*, *Many Voices: Pastoral Psychotherapy and Theology in Relational Perspective*, and *Shared Wisdom: Use of the Self in Pastoral Care and Counseling*. An Episcopal priest and pastoral psychotherapist, Dr. Cooper-White is a clinical Fellow in the American Association of Pastoral Counselors. She serves on the Steering Committee of the Psychology, Culture, and Religion Group of the American Academy of Religion, and the Editorial Board of the *Journal of Pastoral Theology*.

Rev. Dr. Kenneth Dobson is counselor to the President of Payap University. He came to Thailand in 1965 and is living in Chiang Mai with his Thai family. He was a pastor to pastors in the Church of Christ in Thailand and interviewed hundreds of pastors and seminary students for this article.

Rev. Dr. Sally B. Dolch pastors two congregations in the Peninsula-Delaware Conference of the United Methodist Church. She is a member of the CARE Team for clergy sexual misconduct response and the Interagency Sexual Ethics Task Force of the General Commission on the Status and Role of Women of the United Methodist Church. Her first career as a social worker (1975–2002) included community advocacy for domestic violence and sexual assault and the development of a Child Advocacy Center. Her dissertation was on the topic of her article here: *Healing the Breach: Response Team Intervention in United Methodist Congregations* (Wesley Theological Seminary, 2010).

Cléo Fatoorehchi, a French intern at IPS United Nations office, worked with the International Association of Women Judges (IAWJ) to shed light on the worrying issue of sextortion, while covering the Fifty-Fifth United Nations Commission on the Status of Women at New York, 2011. A political science student of Aix-en-Provence, France, she focuses her research and writing on gender issues and deepening her work with women's organizations. Her internship within the IPS also allowed her to report on sex trafficking, rapes, the female role in the Egyptian revolution and the fate of Afghan women.

Rev. Dr. Marie M. Fortune. Since 1976, Marie Fortune has been a pioneer in the field of religion and domestic violence and a leading national expert in the United States on sexual exploitation by religious leaders. She is the Founder and Senior Analyst at FaithTrust Institute. Fortune is an ordained pastor in the United Church of Christ as well as an author, educator, practicing ethicist and theologian. She is the author of *Is Nothing Sacred?* (the story of a pastor, the women he sexually abused and the congregation he nearly destroyed), *Sexual Violence: The Unmentional Sin* and *Love Does No Harm: Sexual Ethics for the Rest of Us.* She served on the National Advisory Council on Violence against Women for the U.S. Department of Justice from 1994–2002 and also on the Defense Task Force on Domestic Violence for the US Defense Department from 2000-2003. She was the editor of the *Journal of Religion and Abuse* from 2000-2008.

Dr. Diana Garland is inaugural Dean of the School of Social Work, Baylor University, Waco, Texas, where she has served on the faculty since 1997. Her newest book is *Inside Out Families: Living the Faith Together*, a result of a research project identifying community service as the most significant contributor to a growing faith among children, adults, and families. She is author, co-author, or editor of 17 other books. She is known for her leadership with congregations and religious organizations in family and community ministry and for her research on the faith life of families.

Amanda Gearing is an award-winning journalist who has worked in Australia and the UK. She established and headed *The Courier-Mail*'s Toowoomba bureau from 1997-2007. In 2002 she received one of Queensland's major media awards: Best News Report, All Media. For the past nine years Amanda has supported several victims of sexual crimes by clergy through criminal cases, church tribunals and civil actions. She has presented papers at major child protection conferences in Sydney and Brisbane and advocates for law reform to improve child protection legislation in Australia. Amanda is currently studying law.

Rex Host is a long-time parishioner of the Baptist churches in Australia and a strong advocate of justice for victims abused by church leaders. He is based in Joondalup, Australia.

Christine Housel is the General Secretary of World Student Christian Federation(WSCF). She is a theology graduate of the Yale School of Divinity. Prior to her work at WSCF, she served in several other capacities in Europe, including, among others, communications consultant to indigenous representatives to the U.N. in Geneva and youth ministries coordinator for the Convocation of American Churches in Europe, in Geneva and Paris.

Rev. Susan Jamison is an ordained Elder in the Susquehanna Conference (Pennsylvania) of the United Methodist Church and has served as pastor of several churches. She is currently in an Extension Ministry Appointment with Albright Care Services (ACS) as the Director of the Annual Fund and Community Relations. ACS provides senior health care and housing. She received the Master of Divinity from Wesley Theological Seminary in Washington, D.C.

Desiree' Kameka is from Miami, Florida.

Victor Kaonga is a global broadcast journalist and heads the Trans World Radio Malawi. He was appointed as a Mover for Gender Justice by the World Council of Churches for his weekly radio column aimed at encouraging gender justice. His radio column is called Bawoli Bane, which means "My Wife." He is married to Thembi. They have four children and live in Malawi's capital city, Lilongwe.

Esther Lubunga Kenge, is former President of the Women Fellowship of the Free Methodist Church in Congo, Annual Conference of Kinshasa. She lectures on theology and development at the Evangelical Seminary of Southern Africa. Esther's doctoral work is on women and peace-building in the Congo. She organizes seminars and workshops on peace and empowerment using contextual Bible study with women from various denominations. In South Africa she works with refugee and abused women and girls in a Shelter called the Haven.

Ann Kennedy is an artist, photographer, and clergy sexual abuse survivor. She is from Ireland.

Dr. Margaret Kennedy is the founder of Minister and Clergy Sexual Abuse Survivors (MACSAS) in the United Kingdom.

Luciano Kovacs is the North American Regional Secretary of the World Student Christian Federation. He previously worked as Social Justice Director for Jan

Hus Presbyterian Church in New York, coordinating its Homeless Outreach and Advocacy, Global Concerns, and Lesbian, Gay Bisexual, and Transgender Advocacy Programmes.

David Masters is a freelance writer based in the United Kingdom. He holds an M.Phil. in Reconciliation Studies, and he worked as the WSCF Europe Regional Secretary in 2010–11.

Rev. Lori McPherson is Clergy on Staff at Metropolitan Community Church of Washington, DC. She is an attorney by trade, having spent five years as a public defender and five years as a local prosecutor, and for the last five years she has worked on the national and international level addressing online child sexual exploitation and sex offender registration. She received her M.Div. from Wesley Theological Seminary, Washington, DC.

Dee Ann Miller is a veteran in the field of clergy sexual abuse of women and responses from churches. She is the author of *How Little We Knew* (1993), her first-person encounter with collusion in the entire system, and *The Truth about Malarkey* (2002). She worked in mental health nursing, especially with other survivors of trauma. Her heritage includes four generations of people in ministry. A former Southern Baptist missionary-nurse and community development worker, she writes as a survivor of sexual assault by a co-worker who also abused adolescent girls.

Dr Fulata L. Moyo is currently World Council of Churches Programme Executive for Women in Church and Society. She is a gender and sexual ethicist, systematic theologian, church historian, and gender and women's human rights activist-scholar. She obtained her doctorate from the University of KwaZulu-Natal, South Africa, with grounding studies from Yale University, USA, in sexual ethics, feminist liberation theologies, epidemiology and social scientific research methodologies. She is also the current General Coordinator of the Circle of Concerned African Women Theologians.

Samantha Nelson serves as Vice President and CEO of The Hope of Survivors and speaks internationally on pastoral sexual abuse. She is a member of the American Association of Christian Counselors (AACC), is a Board Certified Biblical Counselor (BCBC) through the International Board of Christian Counselors, and has authored a book for helping victims of abuse, as well as a training manual for peer support groups. Samantha is also a member of the Adventist Association of Family Life Professionals (AAFLP).

Terry O'Neill, a feminist attorney, professor and activist for social justice, was elected president of the National Organization for Women (NOW) in June 2009. A former law professor, O'Neill taught at Tulane University in New Orleans and at the University of California at Davis, where her courses included feminist legal theory and international women's rights law, in addition to corporate law and legal ethics. O'Neill is also skilled political organizer, having worked on such historic campaigns as for Hillary Clinton, Barack Obama, and Louisiana's first woman U.S. senator, Mary Landrieu.

Janejinda Pawadee is a passionate advocate for the rights of women and children. She worked with national and international NGOs on the issues of child rights and sex-trafficking. Her contribution to churches in Thailand and Mekong countries created space for the rights of ethnic minority and migrant workers. She is also a government-licensed social worker for juvenile cases, working with law enforcement officers and legal advisor for the sexually abused women and children. She worked with the Foundation For Children (FFC), the Church of Christ in Thailand (CCT), International Justice Mission (IJM-Thailand) and Christian Conference of Asia (CCA), and she is presently Coordinator of CCA's Mekong Ecumenical Partnership Programme. In her current role, she works in capacity building, human rights advocacy, HIV and AIDS education and sustainable development.

Garry Prior is a British lawyer and financier who has lived and worked in South East Asia for forty years. He has been involved in church governance across denominations in several international churches in Singapore, Kuala Lumpur and Bangkok for over 25 years as a member of the disciplinary body or as an adviser. He has counselled victims, offenders and church bodies. He and his wife Teresa Ch'ng Pek Guat recently celebrated their 40th wedding anniversary.

Dr. Gary Schoener is a clinical psychologist, forensic consultant and expert witness, especially in cases of professional boundary violations and sexual misconduct. His expertise includes 35 years of consultation and training work, and professional presentations throughout the world. He has consulted or testified in more than 1,000 cases of sexual abuse by clergy, evaluated offending clergy, and has handled cases for more than 30 religious denominations. He currently serves as Director of Consultation and Training of the Walk-In Counseling Center, Minneapolis, Minnesota.

Dr. A.W. Richard Sipe is now a fulltime researcher into the sexual and celibate practices of Roman Catholic bishops and priests. He has spent his life searching for the origins, meanings, and dynamics of religious celibacy. His six books including his now-classic *A Secret World* and *Celibacy in Crisis* explore various aspects of the questions about the pattern and practice of religious celibacy. He spent 18 years serving the Church as a Benedictine monk and Catholic priest. In those capacities he was trained to deal with the mental health problems of priests. He and Marianne have been married since 1970 and have one son, a psychiatrist. Both as a priest and married man he has practiced psychotherapy, taught on the faculties of major Catholic seminaries and colleges, lectured in medical schools, and served as a consultant and expert witness in both civil and criminal cases involving the sexual abuse by Catholic priests.

Dr. Darryl W. Stephens is Assistant General Secretary for Advocacy and Sexual Ethics for the General Commission on the Status and Role of Women of the United Methodist Church. He convenes the United Methodist Inter-agency Sexual Ethics Task Force, conducts trainings in misconduct prevention and response throughout the United States of America, and maintains the website www.umsexualethics. org. A former faculty member of Candler School of Theology, Emory University, Atlanta, Georgia USA, he holds a Ph.D. in Christian Ethics from Emory University and is an ordained deacon.

Dr. Martin Weber is Chairman of the Board and Vice President of The Hope of Survivors' Pastoral Education Division. He has served many years as a pastor, most recently in suburban Sacramento, California. He has volunteered as a law enforcement chaplain with special training in critical incident stress management, working closely with crisis victims and police officers. Among his books are his own story of abuse survival, *My Tortured Conscience,* and *Hurt, Healing and Happy Again.* He currently serves as Director of Communication for the Mid-America Union of Seventh-day Adventists. He and his wife, Darlene, have two adult children and live with their four cats in Lincoln, Nebraska.

Part One
Identifying the Problem

1

Historical Reflections on Clergy Sexual Abuse

GARY R. SCHOENER

Attitudes about women go back to Adam and Eve, David and Bathsheba, Tamar and Amnon, and Joseph and Potiphar's wife, just to begin the list.

Historically and even today, women have been blamed for being the cause of inappropriate sex. "Twelve-year-old killed for having sex; her mother is charged" read the headline of an Associated Press story out of Birmingham, Alabama. The brief text told of "a woman angry with her twelve-year-old daughter for having sex." The mother killed her daughter in a particularly gruesome fashion. The story did not reveal with whom the girl had sex or why the anger was not directed at the male who sexually exploited the little girl.

This is a bizarre and troubling story, but sadly it is not a unique one or one without precedent. "Honor killings" of women for extra-marital or pre-marital sex occur routinely in many cultures. Blaming of the girls for the sex is commonplace throughout the world. This context is the background for our failure to respond to the sexual exploitation of girls and women by clergy and other persons in a position of power.

An Ancient Problem

The dilemma of sexual exploitation of women by professionals pre-dates Christianity. The earliest concerns about physician-patient sex in a written text are to be found in the *Corpus Hippocratum*, a body of about 70 medical texts found in the Library of Alexandria in Egypt during the 4th and 5th centuries B.C.E.[1]

It is not known how many of these works can actually be attributed to Hippocrates, who lived from 460 to 370 B.C.E., although it is quite likely that he did not write the most famous item in the *Corpus*, the Hippocratic Oath, usually attributed to him.[2] Both the Oath and *The Physician* discuss sexual intimacy. The *Oath* states in part:

> With purity and holiness I will practice my art. . . . Into whatever house I
> enter I will go into them for the benefit of the sick and will abstain from

every voluntary act of Mischief and Corruption and further from the seduction of females or males, of freemen and slaves.[3]

During the Middle Ages, sexual contact between clergy and congregants was
known but not widely reported. The church took the position that the clerics
were the legal responsibility of the church and thus not subject to secular law.
Prosecutions took place in ecclesiastical courts under canon law.[4] It is unclear
what impact celibacy vows had as they evolved. A number of historians link
these claims on the assets of the church by widows and offspring of priests as
property rights of women and children were gradually recognized in Europe.[5]

The Modern Story

Issues of sexual exploitation of women by professionals emerge in 18th century
literature. Benjamin Franklin headed a Commission of Inquiry in 1784 drawing attention to physicians taking sexual advantage of their patients through the
misuse of mesmerism (hypnosis). In Franklin's secret report to Louis XVI, the
French king, he stated:

> The danger exists. . . since the physician can, if he will, take advantage
> of his patient. . . . Even if we ascribe to him superhuman virtue, since he
> is exposed to emotions which awaken such desires, the imperious law of
> nature will affect his patient, and he is responsible, not merely for his own
> wrong-doing, but for that he may have excited in another.[6]

Perry notes that at "the time the report was written . . . medical doctors enjoyed a
bad reputation in the eyes of a significant segment of the lay public."[7]

In 2003 Karin Gedge published *Without Benefit of Clergy: Women and the
Pastoral Relationship in Nineteenth-Century American Culture*.[8] She examined the
experiences of women with their pastors in the 19th century. She examined some
trials, one of which was the trial of a Methodist pastor in Rhode Island who
was accused of murdering an unmarried mill worker, Sarah Cornell, who had
claimed that he was the father of her child. This case was not only a focus of
major media attention but also led to songs, poems, and even a play. The defense
trashed the victim, impugned her morals, and acquitted the pastor.

Gedge also reviewed the highly publicized ecclesiastical trial of the Right
Reverend Benjamin Onderdonk, Episcopal Bishop of the State of New York.
Four women had accused him of fondling and sexually groping them. In the
absence of the modern concept of sexual harassment, the case ended with a
middle of the road verdict. The bishop was allowed to keep his title and salary
and residence but was required to surrender his duties as bishop.

In yet another case, in 1857 charges of adultery were brought against Isaac Kolloch, a Baptist Pastor in Boston, for committing adultery with a woman parishioner. As usual, the victim was vilified and the pastor acquitted.

Adultery is still a crime in Minnesota and a number of other states. I became aware of this at the sentencing of pastor Robert Eugene Duttona in Nicollet County. To the shock and dismay of many, Judge Noah Rosenbloom sentenced Dutton to 90 days in jail instead of the two-year sentence that was expected, noting that the victim was guilty of adultery. After verifying the accuracy of the newspaper accounts, Ellen Luepker and I filed complaints against Judge Rosenbloom with the Minnesota Board on Judicial Standards. The Board declined to discipline him. In a private phone call the judge also said that it was a less serious crime to rape a married woman than an unmarried one.[9] Judith Janssen, the remarkable woman who was the victim in this case, nonetheless was undaunted and wrote:

> There have been countless times during the past few years when I have cried out to the Lord about our ever moving to St. Peter. I can now gratefully acknowledge that it was in Minnesota, after August 1985, that the abuse occurred. If this had occurred earlier, or in most other states, I might still be struggling to sort out what happened.[10]

Henry Ward Beecher (1813-1887), brother of feminist and author of *Uncle Tom's Cabin*, Harriet Beecher Stowe, was "one of the premier preachers in the late nineteenth century," according to the *Dictionary of Christianity in America*.[11] At the height of his distinguished career and pastoral influence, Beecher counseled ElizabethTilton, the wife of a friend, who was grieving the death of her infant. Beecher sexually exploited Ms. Tilton and cautioned her not to tell anyone about it.[12] In 1872 journalist Victoria Woodhull published the story of the relationship and was sued for libel and jailed. A congregational investigating committee, ignoring "almost irrefutable evidence," not only exonerated Beecher but expressed toward him "sympathy more tender and trust more unbounded" than before.[13] In a sad twist of fate the journalist Victoria Woodhull had a romantic involvement with Mr.Tilton.[14] Elizabeth Tilton was excommunicated in 1878 and died blind and alone. Beecher's career was not significantly affected.[15]

The issue of sexual contact between a pastor and female parishioners was also the subject of a number of works of fiction. In 1850, Nathaniel Hawthorne's *The Scarlet Letter* described the shame of a young woman, Hester Prynne, who was forced to wear the scarlet letter *A* for adulteress after having been made pregnant by a clergyman, Arthur Dimmesdale. The pastor escaped public disgrace but not negative emotional consequences. When Hester inquired as to whether the good works he had done in the church among those who revered him had brought him any comfort, Dimmesdale replied:

> As concerns the good which I may appear to do, I have no faith in it. It must needs be a delusion. What can a ruined soul, like mine, effect towards the redemption of other souls?—or a polluted soul, towards their purification? And as for the people's reverence, would that it were turned to scorn and hatred! Canst thou deem it, Hester, a consolation, that I must stand up in my pulpit, and meet so many eyes turned upward to my face, as if the light of heaven were beaming from it!—and then look inward, and discern the black reality of what they idolize? I have laughed, in bitterness and agony of heart, at the contrast between what I seem and what I am!

And Satan laughs at it![16] Romance novels of the late 19th and 20th centuries typically portray pastors as boyish and innocent men, pursued by women who seek to seduce them and whose clutches they barely managed to escape.[17] For example, Corra Harris's *A Circuit Rider's Wife,* published in 1910 (and serialized in the *Saturday Evening Post* the same year), includes the following narration by Mary, the wife of a Methodist minister:

> When we hear of a minister who has disgraced himself with some female member of his flock, my sympathies are all with the preacher. I know exactly what has happened. Some sad-faced lady who has been "awakened" from a silent, cold, backslidden state by his sermons goes to see him in his church study. (They who build studies for their preachers in the back part of the church surround him with four walls of moral destruction and invite it for him. The place for a minister's study is in his own home, with his wife passing in and out, if he has female spiritual invalids calling on him.)
>
> This lady is perfectly innocent in that she has not considered her moral responsibility to the preacher she is about to victimize. She is very modest, really and truly modest. He is a little on his guard until he discovers this. First, she tells him that she is unhappy at home.
>
> He sees her reduced to tears over her would-be transgressions, and before he considers what he is about he has kissed the "dear child." That is the way it happens nine times out of ten, a good man damned and lost by some frail angel of the church.[18]

Mary nipped one such potential relationship—that between a parishioner and her minister husband, William—in the bud by privately confronting the woman, after having watched with chagrin that:

> William was always cheered and invigorated by her visits. He would come out of his study for tea after her departure, rubbing his hands and prais-

ing the beautiful, spiritual clearness of her mind, which he considered very remarkable in a woman.[19]

Mary proposes a solution to this problem:

> Someone who understands real moral values ought to make a new set of civil laws that would apply to the worst class of criminals in society—not the poor, hungry, simple-minded rogues, the primitive murderers, but the real rotters of honor and destroyers of salvation. Then we should have a very different class of people in the penitentiaries, and not the least numerous among them would be the women who make a religion of sneaking up on the blind male side of good men without a thought of the consequences.[20]

The problem, according to Harris and other authors? Exploitive male clergy? No, seductive women. Although Harris's account was of the 1880s, and published in 1910, it should be noted that it was reissued as *The Circuit Rider's Wife* in 1988 and had a second printing in 1990, so somebody is still reading it. Furthermore, *The Bishop's Mantle,* written almost forty years later by Agnes Turnbull in 1948, contained similar sentiments, describing the struggles of Hilary Laurens, a young minister, who was barely able to escape the clever plotting of predatory women in his congregation:

> In spite of himself he thought of the ministers, from Beecher down, who had had trouble with women. Every city clergyman had to recognize *this menace.* A few to his own knowledge through the years, in spite of their utter innocence, had yet escaped by a hair's breadth. A few here and there had not even escaped. There were always the neurotic women who flocked not only to the psychiatrists but also in almost equal numbers to ministers, pouring out their heart confessions and their fancied ills; there were those pitiable ones in whose minds religion and sex had become confused and intermingled; there were those who quite starkly fell in love with a clergyman and wanted love from him in return. Yes, a man of God had to be constantly on his guard in connection with *this problem of women.*[21]

Counselor Abuse and Modern Psychiatry

In his classic 1917 *Introductory Lectures in Psychoanalysis,* Sigmund Freud noted the romantic and erotic feelings his female patients exhibited toward him, labeling it *transference.*[22] Freud clearly indicated that the therapist should not take advantage of the patient's "longing for love" and should abstain from sexual involvement. Freud also noted that the therapist had to struggle with his own countertransference love feelings.

The psychoanalyst Carl Jung had a romantic affair with Sabina Spielrein, whom he treated from 1905 to 1909. She was 19 years old when she began her analysis. Subsequently she became a physician and in 1912 joined the Vienna Psychoanalytic Society.[23] In a 1909 letter to Sigmund Freud, dated 4 June, Jung indicated that Spielrein was "systematically planning [his] seduction."[24] Freud's response, dated 7 June, was supportive, noting that while he himself had "never been taken in quite so badly," he had "come very close to it a number of times and had a narrow escape."[25] The blame was Spielrein's: "The way these women manage to charm us with every conceivable psychic perfection until they have attained their purpose is one of nature's greatest spectacles."[26]

Jung replied to Freud on 21 June that he had met with Spielrein and discovered that she had not been the source of the rumors about their relationship and indicates remorse about "the sins" he had committed:

> When the situation had become so tense that the continued preservation of the relationship could be rounded out only by sexual acts, I defended myself in a manner that cannot be justified morally. Caught in my delusion that I was the victim of the sexual wiles of my patient, I wrote to her mother that I was not the gratifier of her daughter's sexual desires but merely her doctor, and that she should free me from her. In view of the fact that the patient had shortly before been my friend and enjoyed my full confidence, my action was a piece of knavery which I very reluctantly confess to you as my father.[27]

Jung had written to Sabina Spielrein's mother, indicating that he had moved from doctor to friend "the more easily" because he had not charged a fee, and then made a proposition that he would come to regret, that if she wished him "to adhere strictly to [his] role as doctor," she should pay him "a fee as suitable recompense for [his] trouble."[28]

Freud then reported to Jung on 30 June that he had written to Sabina Spielrein's mother, as Jung asked him to do, and that "the matter has ended in a manner satisfactory to all." He told Jung not to fault himself for drawing Freud into the situation, asserting that "it was not your doing but hers." [29] For both Jung and Freud, the problem is clear: seductive women.

Kerr, in *A Most Dangerous Method* (1993), writes of this history:

> Jung was scarcely the only person to become involved with a patient. Gross's exploits were legendary, Stekel had long enjoyed a reputation as a 'seducer,' Jones was paying blackmail money to a former patient, and even good Pastor Pfister was lately being entraced by one of his charges. Indeed, the most extraordinary entanglement was Ferenczi's, the amiable Hungarian having taken into analysis the daughter of the woman he was having an affair with and then fallen in love with the girl.[30]

Professionals Discover the Issue

The 1970s also saw the advent of the self-report survey of professional groups with the publication of Kardener, Fuller, & Mensh's (1973) study of a sample of 1,000 physicians in Los Angeles County. Their finding that 10 percent of psychiatrists and other physicians acknowledged erotic contact with clients and that 5 percent acknowledged sexual intercourse, established the seriousness and scope of the problem and presaged the ensuing professional debate, as well as a large number of self-report surveys.[31] In March 1973 the case of *Roy v. Hartogs* was tried in New York City. Julie Roy, the plaintiff, charged Dr. Renatus Hartogs, a psychiatrist with good credentials and the author of a column for *Cosmopolitan* magazine, with sexual exploitation. She won the suit and the next year co-authored a book, *Betrayal,* which was later made into a television movie of the same title.[32] The broad publicity of the case led to many other clients coming forward.

A major discussion of therapist-client sex occurred in May 1976 at the annual convention of the American Psychiatric Association. The next year a national survey of psychologists was published whose findings mirrored those of Kardener, Fuller, & Mensh,[33] and in 1978 a California Psychological Association Task Force undertook a large-scale survey of psychologists concerning their knowledge of such cases.

For the most part, pastors were not the subjects of such surveys till later. Richard Blackmon, in a 1984 unpublished doctoral dissertation at Fuller Theological Seminary, surveyed clergy in four denominations–Presbyterian, United Methodist, Episcopalian, and Assembly of God–and found that 39 percent acknowledged sexual contact with a congregant and 12.7 percent sexual intercourse with a congregant. These figures are far higher than self-reported data from physicians or mental health professionals. In addition, 76.5 percent indicated that they knew of a pastor who had sex with a congregant—again, a higher number than in secular professions studied.

A full 23 percent of pastors who responded to a 1987 survey in *Christianity Today* indicated that they had engaged in inappropriate sexual behavior after having entered into the work of ministry. And 12 percent admitted to sex with someone other than their spouse. A survey of Southern Baptist pastors found that more than 70 percent knew of pastors who had sex with a congregant, although only 6 percent admitted that they had done so. An additional 4 percent admitted sex with a former congregant.

Charles Rassieur wrote a book, *The Problem Clergymen Don't Talk About* (1977), but it was aimed at seminarians and clergy and known only to them. Don Baker's *Beyond Forgiveness* (1984) was published by a small religious press in Oregon. It told the story of a pastor who had sexually exploited a number of women. The sexual exploitation of women was examined in a Minnesota book: *Sexual Assault and Abuse: A Handbook for Clergy and Religious Professionals,* edited by Mary Pellauer, Barbara Chester, and Jane Boyajian. Mary was a leader in working on these issues in the ELCA, Barbara headed the Rape Counseling Center in Minneapolis, and Jane was a theologian and ethicist.

Other books dealing with sexual exploitation of women in Protestant or Catholic settings followed. Eventually there was a flurry of books about the sexual abuse of children in churches and religious institutions, many of which were focused on the abuse of boys. Websites evolved. Many can be found through Advocateweb: www.advocateweb.org. Advocateweb is focused on sexual exploitation and abuse of women by all types of helping professionals. Those who access its Forum are typically women who have been victimized by male or female professionals, including clergy.

The Awareness Center is a resource in the Jewish community. It is at www. awarenesscenter.org. Charlotte Schwab wrote about rabbinic abuse of women in *Sex, Lies, and Rabbis Breaking a Sacred Trust* (2002).

Evolving Popular, Legislative, and Institutional Responses

Newspaper advice columns also reveal attitudes. In 1986 Ann Landers published a letter from a man, "More than I Needed to Know in Panama City," who learned on his honeymoon that his wife had slept with five men who were at their wedding *including the minister who married them.* Among other things, Ann advised: "And for heaven's sake, tell Sally to keep her mouth shut. The minister doesn't need the publicity."

Landers withdrew this advice when she published a follow-up letter from "Disappointed in Detroit": "For 32 years I was married to a minister who was protected by people who also kept their mouths shut. In the meantime, my husband was taking advantage of young women to whom he should have been ministering. If people had not remained silent, he would have been removed from his job. The next result was that he caused irreparable harm to all of those who believed he was a servant of God."

In 1989 Landers published a letter from "A Crushed Christian in California" who said that an associate pastor began courting her as soon as he learned of a recent large insurance settlement she had received. As soon as they married, he began dominating her life, frequently citing "God's Will" as a rationale. She wrote: "Using 'God' to control, manipulate, bully and extort is cruel and sadistic. My emotional scars will take years to heal and I may never fully trust a minister or church again."

In recent years advice columns have given far better advice regarding sexual exploitation of women by clergy, shown greater sophistication with the issue and displayed values sensitive to exploited women when topic has come up.

Women who have been sexually exploited, as well as concerned professionals, began seeking remedies through media attention and changes in public policy. In 1984 Wisconsin criminalized therapist-client sex, although the statute specifically did not include clergy. That same year the Minnesota legislature created a Task Force on Sexual Exploitation by Counselors and Psychotherapists which examined sexual exploitation by professionals, including clergy.

In 1985 Minnesota criminalized therapist-client sex, making it a felony. This included sexual contact by clergy. To date more than twenty states have criminalized therapist-client sex. The majority of them include clergy among the counselors.[34] Most of those who testified at hearings in Minnesota and elsewhere were women victimized as adults or adolescents.

In 1992, after a pastor successfully used the "spiritual counseling defense," the Minnesota Legislature expanded the criminal statute specifically to include spiritual counseling. Pastoral sexual conduct with counselees has been a crime in Minnesota for over a decade. However, it requires a one-on-one counseling, it cannot be simply as a pastor. The only other state which has such a law is Texas. It was signed into law by George W. Bush.

In the 1980s interdenominational task forces in several states examined sexual misconduct by clergy with both child and adult counselees or parishioners. The Washington Council of Churches issued a report on *Sexual Contact by Pastors and Pastoral Counselors in Professional Relationships* in 1984 and the Minnesota Interfaith Committee on Sexual Exploitation by Clergy published *Sexual Exploitation by Clergy: Reflections and Guidelines for Religious Leaders* in 1989.

That same year Rev. Marie Fortune's book *Is Nothing Sacred?* was published. She challenged religious communities to deal more effectively with sexual misconduct in the church. Dr. Peter Rutter's *Sex in the Forbidden Zone* (1989) generated considerable discussion and media coverage in North America and brought about in incredible response from many victims/survivors of sexual misconduct by professionals. As a result of reading this book, hundreds of people have contacted our center, the Walk-In Center, about misconduct by therapists and clergy.

The Minnesota Task Force on Sexual Exploitation by Counselors and Therapists published a manual for the State of Minnesota titled *It's Never OK.*

Our own work and that of these task forces evolved to examine sexual exploitation by all counseling professions, both secular ones as well as clergy. This is very different from the revelations in the 1990s about sexual abuse of boys by Catholic priests. LINK UP and SNAP originally were focused mostly on one denomination—Roman Catholicism—and heavily focused on abuse of minors. Originally, one movement focused on women victims of misconduct by a wide range of professionals while the other movement focused on religious predators and the abuse especially of boys.

On June 5 and 6, 1986, a national conference entitled "It's Never OK" was held in Minneapolis and co-sponsored by the Continuing Education and Extension division of the University of Minnesota and the Minnesota Task Force on Sexual Exploitation by Counselors and Therapists.[35] For the most part, the program examined sexual exploitation by psychotherapists and clergy. The conference drew 250 people from around the United States.

The next conference was not until 1992. It, too, was in Minneapolis, and was co-sponsored by the Walk-In Counseling Center and several other groups. It drew more than 650 people from around the world. The book *Breach of Trust* was something akin to a proceedings for this conference.[36] In 1994 another such conference was held in Toronto, Ontario, and drew about 600 people and in 1998 another one in Chestnut Hill, Massachusetts.

There have been regional conferences in Canada and in Houston, Texas, and workshops in a number of places. Two very large Australia-New Zealand conferences have been held in Sydney (1994) and Melbourne (1996) on sexual exploitation of women by professionals. In Switzerland, a group called AGAVA held major conferences in 2001 and 2002.

Rev. Marie Fortune and the Center for the Prevention of Sexual and Domestic Violence (now the FaithTrust Institute) in Seattle have sponsored victim retreats around the United States. A number of other advocates have done this periodically, sometimes for victims of clergy and sometimes for victims of both clergy and therapists. BASTA, run by Estelle Disch in the Boston area, held such retreats for a number of years.[37]

Jeanette Milgrom of the Walk-In Counseling Center began the first support groups for women victims of sexual exploitation by counselors in 1976. In 1979 Ellen Luepker began offering support groups through Minneapolis Family and Children's Service.[38] She continued this work for many years when she established a private practice.

By the end of the 1980s and beginning of the 1990s a number of church denominations had developed or were working on policies and guidelines for handling complaints of sexual misconduct by clergy. A large percentage of cases were those of female parishioners or counselees who had come forward to complain of sexual exploitation by male clergy. One issue is the responsibility of the church for the pastor's misconduct. Minnesota passed Minnesota Statutes 148.A, which outlines the duties of an employer of someone who might do counseling. This radically affected churches. It includes a requirement that they (1) check at least five years back for any information from past employers concerning sex with clients or attempts at it; and (2) that when asked they pass the information on. If they fail to do so, they can be liable for future damages. Case law has basically established that there can be a failure to supervise as well as other employer-related failures. Under some circumstances a bishop can be held personally accountable for action or inaction after the fact.

2

Sexual Abuse by Religious Leaders

Marie M. Fortune

Religious institutions, both formal and informal, now face the consequences of long-standing professional misconduct involving sexual abuse by their leaders. Their history of nondisclosure to authorities, and nonaction (except to protect the clergy) is now reaping a whirlwind.

The long-standing problem of sexual abuse of congregants by clergy and religious leaders has finally made its way into public consciousness, largely due to the persistence of the media. Although religious leaders are not the only professionals to exploit those who seek their help, when they do so they betray both a helping relationship and a spiritual relationship, which can carry heavy consequences for the victims. No denomination or creed is immune from this professional pastoral problem: religious leaders, whether Protestant or Catholic, Buddhist or Jewish, Muslim or of the Native traditions, occupy positions of trust, which can easily be abused. Nor is this problem new: The historical record suggests that for many centuries some male religious leaders have used their positions to gain sexual access to women and children, and institutions of organized religion have tolerated their behavior. This particular expression of sexual violence, although long hidden, has now become public. The administrative bodies that train, oversee, ordain, and supervise religious leaders should have a primary responsibility to do all they can to ensure that faith communities and places of worship are safe for all participants.

The Problem

When a pastoral relationship becomes a sexual one, a boundary is violated, whether the context is a clergy-congregant, a counseling, a staff supervisory, or a mentor relationship. When a religious leader sexualizes the pastoral or counseling relationship, it is similar to the violation of the therapeutic relationship by a therapist. When the religious leader sexualizes the supervisory or mentor relationship with a staff member or student, it is similar to sexual harassment in the workplace, and the principles of workplace harassment apply. When a child or teenager is the object of the sexual contact, the situation is one of pedophilia or child sexual abuse, which is by definition not only unethical and abusive but criminal. Likewise, if the boundary violation is an assault, it is the crime of rape. Although most often the boundary violation is not forced or coerced but manipulated with an illusion of consent, this does not mitigate the damage it causes.

Sexual contact by religious leaders and pastoral counselors with congregants/ clients undercuts an otherwise effective pastoral relationship and violates the trust necessary for that relationship. It is not the sexual contact per se that is problematic but the fact that the sexual activity takes place within the pastoral relationship. The violation of this particular boundary changes the nature of the relationship and has enormous potential to cause harm. The behaviors that occur in sexual violation of boundaries include but are not limited to sexual comments or suggestions such as jokes, innuendoes, or invitations, touching, fondling, seduction, kissing, intercourse, molestation, and rape. There may be only one incident or a series of incidents or an ongoing intimate relationship.

Sexual behavior in pastoral relationships is an instance of professional misconduct that is often minimized or ignored. This is not just an affair, although it may involve an ongoing sexual relationship with a client or congregant. It is not merely adultery, although adultery may be a consequence if the religious leader/counselor or congregant/client is in a committed relationship. And it is not just a momentary lapse of judgment by the religious leader or counselor; often there is a recurring pattern of misuse of the pastoral role by a cleric who seems neither to comprehend nor to care about the damaging effects it may have on the congregant/client.

Research on sexual involvement between clergy and congregants is sparse, but research and media reports of charges and civil or criminal actions suggest that between 10 and 20 percent of clergy violate sexual boundaries in their professional relationships. Although the vast majority of pastoral offenders in reported cases are heterosexual males and the vast majority of victims are heterosexual females, neither gender nor sexual orientation excludes anyone from the risk of offending (clergy) or from the possibility of being taken advantage of (congregants/clients) in the pastoral or counseling relationship. Some of the conduct can be described as wandering. Religious leaders who wander and violate sexual boundaries are often ill-trained and insensitive and use poor judgment, with complete disregard for the impact on the congregant, student, or client. If called to account and given training and supervision, wanderers may be able to return to responsible ministry. At the other end of the spectrum, however, are religious leaders whose behavior can be described as predatory. Whether they offend against children, youths, or adults, these leaders intentionally target vulnerable people, grooming them and manipulating them into crossing sexual boundaries. Some may be clinically diagnosed as sex offenders. Some may be criminally prosecuted. Most are sociopathic and thus accomplished at manipulating the system in which they operate. Once identified, they should be removed from any role of trust and responsibility for others and, if appropriate, prosecuted. They cannot be restored to responsible ministry.

Consequences

Sexual contact with their religious leader or counselor has a profound psychological effect on congregants and clients. Initially, clients/congregants may feel flattered by the special attention and may even see themselves as consenting to the activity. Frequently, however, the congregants/clients have sought pastoral care during a time of crisis and are emotionally vulnerable.[1] Eventually they begin to realize that they are being denied a much-needed pastoral relationship and begin to feel taken advantage of. Additionally, the victims of clerical abuse may feel betrayed, victimized, confused, fearful, embarrassed, or ashamed, and may blame themselves; at this point they are not likely to discuss the situation with anyone and so remain isolated. They are at risk for depression, substance abuse, or suicide. If and when anger finally surfaces, they may be ready to break the silence and take some action on their own behalf and on behalf of others. Once having disclosed their situation, survivors depend heavily for their healing on the response of the institution or faith group. Too often survivors of clerical abuse meet a response of disbelief, blame, and ostracism. This will revictimize them, since they are abandoned by their faith community. A response of support and compassion and a willingness to hold religious leaders accountable can help survivors to heal from the abuse.

Spiritually, the consequences are also profound; the psychological pain is magnified and takes on cosmic proportions. The congregants/clients are not only betrayed by someone representing God but also feel betrayed by God and their faith community. Religious leaders/counselors are very powerful and can easily manipulate their victims not only psychologically but also spiritually and morally. Religious leaders are reported to have justified their boundary-crossing behavior in these ways:

- "He said that love can never be wrong; that God had brought us together."
- "He said we should sin boldly so that grace might abound."
- "She said that ministry was mutual and our relationship was mutual. So she shared her problems with me and the sex followed from that."

- "I was learning about God for the first time. He took me seriously. I went along with the sex so that I could continue to learn from him." The result for congregants or students is enormous confusion and guilt; this psychological crisis becomes a crisis of faith as well, with very high stakes.

Manipulation by religious leaders or pastoral counselors compromises the moral agency and otherwise good judgment of congregants. If the person they rely on as a moral guide explains away any moral question they may have about engaging in sexual activity and requires them to keep it secret so they are not able to check this out with someone else who might help them see more clearly what is happening, it is very easy to be deceived. The result is that many survivors of clergy abuse end up feeling stupid and blaming themselves, when in fact someone they trusted stole their moral agency from them. Entire congregations are also devastated by clergy sexual abuse. With or without disclosure, the impact of boundary violations ripples through the membership. The whole congregation feels their trust has been betrayed.

Consequences can include loss of faith, financial liability, and loss of members, and the residue lasts for years unless the congregation has an opportunity to confront the truth and find healing. Finally, the consequences are also profound for the religious leaders and their families. Not only is there the internal betrayal of their vocation, with disclosure there may well be loss of employment, status, and benefits, or imprisonment. The profession as a whole also faces consequences. Daily reports of clergy members being arrested and new civil actions against the governing bodies of religious institutions seriously compromise the credibility of all religious leaders. While not all religious leaders are engaged in boundary violations, all bear the burden of distrust created by the misconduct of a minority.

An Ethical Analysis

The ethical analysis of sexual abuse and boundary violation by religious leaders has been woefully inadequate in many circles. For example, in the proposed revisions to the U.S. Roman Catholic Bishops' Dallas Policy (2002) on the sexual abuse of children by priests, the bishops directly tie the definition of sexual abuse to a moral standard based on the Sixth Commandment in the Hebrew scriptures: "You shall not commit adultery." The average layperson would rightly ask, "I thought adultery was about adults having sex with someone they are not married to. What does sexual abuse of kids have to do with adultery?"

The fundamental ethical question is, why is it wrong for an adult to be sexual with a child or teen? The answer is not a difficult one: It is a betrayal of trust, a misuse of adult authority, taking advantage of a child's vulnerability, sexual activity in the absence of meaningful consent; it is, in other words, rape. When an ordained member of the clergy has been sexual with a child, it is also a betrayal of the role of the pastor. Our job as clergy is to nurture the flock, to protect them when they are vulnerable, and to empower them in their lives—especially children and youth. Our people assume they can trust us not to harm them, because we are clergy. Sexual abuse betrays that trust.

The bishops turned to the wrong commandment. Instead of the sixth, they should have gone to the seventh: "You shall not steal." To steal is to take something that doesn't belong to you. To sexually abuse a child is to steal the child's innocence and future, often with profound and tragic consequences. When an acknowledged pedophile priest can say that he didn't see what was wrong with his behavior with a child because he had been taught not to have sex with adult women, we can begin to see the inadequacy of this ethical analysis. The sexual abuse of a child or teen is about the misuse of power by the adult. It is about theft: taking advantage of a child's naiveté, stealing his or her future.

Clarity of ethical analysis is necessary to help shape an effective response to disclosures of abuse. It is a violation of professional ethics for any person in a pastoral role of leadership or pastoral counseling (clergy or lay) to engage in sexual contact or sexualized behavior with a congregant, client, employee, or student, whether adult, teen, or child, within the professional pastoral or supervisory relationship. It is wrong because sexual activity in this context is exploitative and abusive:

• *Role violation.* The pastoral relationship involves certain role expectations. The religious leader/counselor is expected to make available certain resources, talents, knowledge, and expertise that will serve the best interest of the congregant, client, staff member, or student. Sexual contact is not part of the pastoral professional role. Important boundaries within the pastoral or counseling relationship are crossed and as a result trust is betrayed. The sexual nature of this boundary violation is significant only in that the sexual context is one of great vulnerability for most people. However, the essential harm is that of betrayal of trust.

• *Misuse of authority and power.* The role of religious leader/counselor carries with it authority and power, and the attendant responsibility to use this power to benefit the people who call on the religious leader/counselor for service. This power can easily be misused, as is the case when a member of the clergy uses (intentionally or unintentionally) his or her authority to initiate or pursue sexual contact with a congregant or client. Even if it is the congregant who sexualizes the relationship, it is still the religious leader's responsibility to maintain the boundaries of the pastoral relationship and not pursue a sexual relationship.

• *Taking advantage of vulnerability.* The congregant, client, employee, or student is by definition vulnerable to the religious leader/counselor. She or he has fewer resources and less power, and when a member of the clergy takes advantage of this vulnerability to gain sexual access, the clergy member violates the mandate to protect the vulnerable from harm.[2]

• *Absence of meaningful consent.* In order to consent fully to sexual activity, an individual must have a choice and the relationship must be one of mutuality and equality; hence, meaningful consent requires the absence of fear or of even the subtlest coercion. There is always an imbalance of power and thus inequality between a person in the pastoral role and those whom he or she serves or supervises. Even in a relationship between two persons who see themselves as consenting adults, the difference in role precludes the possibility of meaningful consent.

An Institutional Crisis

Religious institutions, both formal and informal, face the consequences of long-standing professional misconduct involving sexual abuse by their leaders. Their history of nondisclosure to authorities, and inaction (except to protect the clergy), is reaping a whirlwind. The enormous cost in legal fees and settlements is but a material indicator of the depth of damage done to the institutions and their members. Some dioceses are facing bankruptcy and others are cutting back funds for social programs. The history of religious bodies' responses to complaints of sexual abuse and professional misconduct suggests that they have followed an institutional protection agenda, which, ironically, has not worked. Nonetheless, it has dominated the strategies of many governing bodies.

An institutional protection agenda uses scripture to avoid action: for example, "Judge not that you not be judged." It uses language to confuse and distort reality: "It was just an indiscretion and it only happened once." It instructs its legal counsel to protect the organization from victims and survivors. It develops policies whose sole purpose is to protect the institution from liability. It urges liturgies that immediately focus on forgiveness, which will only serve to "heal the wound lightly." It allocates funds to defend the institution in civil litigation while it shuns victims and survivors and attempts to silence them. It resists reform at all costs.

But there is another possible agenda, one more congruent with the teaching and values of religious organizations. A justice-making agenda uses scripture to name the sin and lift up victims: for example, "It would be better for you if a millstone were hung around your neck and you were thrown into the sea than for you to cause one of these little ones to stumble." It uses language to clarify: "This is sexual abuse of the most vulnerable by the powerful. It is a sin and a crime." It instructs its legal counsel to find ways to make justice for survivors and to hold perpetrators accountable. It develops and implements policies whose purpose is to protect the people from their institution and from those who would misuse their power. It encourages liturgies, when the time is right, that name the sin, confess culpability, remember the victims, and celebrate justice really made—all of which allow for healing and restoration. It allocates its funds for restitution to victims and survivors and for education and training for prevention. It does not look for a scapegoat but looks inside itself with a critical eye, focusing on power as the true issue. It seeks out those who have been harmed, thanks them for their courage in disclosing their abuse, and supports them in their healing. It has the courage to ask what reforms are needed in order to be faithful to the most important values that the religious organization espouses.

Some Roman Catholic bishops and cardinals in the United States have argued that their early management of the reports of priests' sexual abuse of children was sincerely motivated by their desire to protect the church from scandal. This translated as protecting priests from the consequences of their misconduct, keeping secrets, and limiting the financial liability of the institution. Ironically, their mismanagement now undermines the credibility of all priests, compromises the image and moral capital of the whole church, and will cost far more financially than it needed to. In other words, even the institutional protection agenda didn't protect the institution in the long run. The betrayal of any helping relationship is about the misuse of power, in this case to violate sexual boundaries. It is the importance of power in a helping relationship that led Hippocrates to formulate the Hippocratic Oath more than two thousand years ago and commit physicians "to keep [patients] from harm and injustice" with these words: "Whatever houses I may visit, I will come for the benefit of the sick, remaining free of all intentional injustice, of all mischief and in particular of sexual relations with both female and male persons, be they free or slaves." He was concerned about the helper taking advantage of the vulnerable and so offered these boundaries to remind any who would serve others of their responsibilities to protect the vulnerable.

Since the mid-1980s in the United States, the discussion of the problem of ministerial misconduct has expanded; disclosures by victims/survivors have increased; lawsuits against churches and synagogues, denominations and movements, as well as pastoral counselors, have multiplied. A crisis has come to light that now challenges the professional credibility of all religious leaders and religious institutions. A number of denominations, at the national and regional levels, have moved to develop policy and procedures as they are being faced with an increasing number of complaints.

More research projects are under way. Codes of ethics have been written or revised by professional organizations. Some attention is beginning to be focused at the seminary level on preparing clergy and pastoral counselors to lessen their risk of violating the integrity of the ministerial relationship. Seminaries are key to preventing sexual abuse and boundary violations by religious leaders. Training for ministry and leadership must address professional ethics, boundaries, power, and authority. Students should be supported in exploring their own histories, especially family-of-origin issues of abuse or dysfunction, and their own healing. But religious institutions also share responsibility for effectively screening candidates, supervising and evaluating their work, and if necessary removing them if they are shown to be abusive.

People who approach a helping professional such as a religious leader should be able to trust that they will be safe and that their sexual and emotional boundaries will not be violated. This requires well-trained, sensitive, committed religious leaders whose first concern is the well-being of their congregants, students, or clients. Too often in the past, religious leaders, out of ignorance or with intention, have taken advantage of the vulnerabilities of those who came to them for help. If a religious institution or organization gives credentials to its leaders, allowing them to teach or practice ministry, then it also has the responsibility to remove those credentials when it discovers that a leader cannot be trusted and is doing harm in the community. Only this social contract can sustain the professional credibility of religious leaders, institutions, and organizations.

3

Clergy Sexual Misconduct

Diana R. Garland

This research study[1] involved two companion projects: (1) a national random survey to determine the prevalence of clergy sexual misconduct (CSM) with adults and (2) a qualitative study of three groups of women and men: (a) those who self-identified as survivors who had been the objects of CSM, (b) family or friends of survivors, and (c) offenders who had themselves committed CSM. The goal of both projects was to define the scope and nature of CSM, so that effective prevention strategies can be proposed for the protection of religious leaders and congregants.

General Statistics of the Research

• National, random survey conducted in 2008 with 3,559 respondents
• Phone interviews with 46 persons who had experienced clergy sexual misconduct as adults, representing 17 different Christian and Jewish religious affiliations
• Phone interviews with 15 persons who were second-hand victims of CSM (husbands, friends and other church staff members); and with 21 experts (non-offending religious leaders, researchers, and professionals who provide care for survivors and offenders.

The Prevalence of CSM

We used the 2008 General Social Survey (GSS) to estimate the prevalence of clergy sexual misconduct. This is an in-person survey of a nationally representative sample of noninstitutionalized English- or Spanish-speaking adults, conducted by National Opinion Research Center at the University of Chicago. The 2008 survey included 3559 respondents. Although the GSS is an in-person interview, the questions we developed specifically for this project were self-administered, making it easier for respondents to report potentially painful or embarrassing experiences.

Clergy Sexual Misconduct Was Defined in This Study

Minister, priests, rabbis, or other clergypersons or religious leaders who make sexual advances or propositions to persons in the congregations they serve who are not their spouses or significant others.

Results of Those Surveyed

• More than 3 percent of women who had attended a congregation in the past month reported that they had been the object of CSM at some time in their adult lives

• 92 percent of these sexual advances had been made in secret, not in open dating relationships

• 67 percent of the offenders were married to someone else at the time of the advance

• In the average American congregation of 400 persons, with women representing, on average, 60 percent of the congregation, there are an average of 7 women who have experienced clergy sexual misconduct

• Of the entire sample, 8 percent report having known about CSM occurring in a congregation they have attended. Therefore, in the average American congregation of 400 congregants, there are, on average, 32 persons who have experienced CSM in their community of faith.

Of course, CSM does not occur evenly across congregations, but these statistics demonstrate the widespread nature of CSM and refutes the commonly held belief that it is a case of a few charismatic and powerful leaders preying on vulnerable followers. In the nonrandom qualitative study that occurred concurrently with the survey, survivors hailed from 17 different Christian and Jewish affiliations: Catholic, Baptist, Methodist, Lutheran, Seventh Day Adventist, Disciples of Christ, Latter Day Saints, Apostolic, Calvary Chapel, Christian Science, Church of Christ, Episcopal, Friends (Quaker), Mennonite, Evangelical, Nondenominational (Christian), and Reform Judaism.

How CSM Happens

In the second phase of the project, we analyzed phone interviews with 46 persons who as adults had experienced a sexual encounter or relationship with a religious leader. We also interviewed 15 others who had experienced the effects of those sexual encounters (husbands, friends and other staff members in the congregation), as well as two offending leaders. We identified subjects for this study using networks of professionals, web sites, and media stories about the project. Most of the offenders of the interview subjects were male, but two were female. Considering that most religious leaders are male, it is significant that we found both male and female offenders, and offenders who committed hetero-sexual, gay and lesbian sexual misbehavior.

We used the software package *Atlas-Ti* to code the interview transcripts and then to identify six common themes that describe the social characteristics of the congregations in which clergy sexual misconduct (CSM) occurs. Those themes include:

1. *Family members, friends, and victims ignored warning signs.* Religious lead-ers acted inappropriately in public as well as private settings, but in a culture that has no cognitive categories for understanding or explaining clergy misconduct as anything other than an "affair," observers mistrusted their own judgment, perhaps considering themselves "hypersensitive," particularly since the behavior was committed by a trusted leader. First indicators of CSM were thus ignored.

2. *Niceness culture:* American culture expects persons to be "nice" to one another, particularly those we know and respect, and particularly in a congrega-tion. "Nice" means not being confrontational, giving the other the "benefit of the doubt," and overlooking social indiscretions in order to avoid embarrass-ment. Even when family members, friends, and victims knew about or suspected CSM or behavior leading to CSM, they did not speak about their observations.

3. *Ease of private communication:* E-mail and cell phones have replaced mailed letters and phone calls to the family household. An intimate relation-ship between leader and congregant can develop via e-mail and cell phones with complete invisibility to family and community.

4. *No oversight:* Religious leaders often answer to no one about their daily activities and are free to move about the community and to maintain an office that is isolated from observation.

5. *Multiple roles:* Religious leaders engage in multiple roles with congregants in addition to their role as leader, including counselor and personal friend. They obtain knowledge about congregants' personal lives and struggles that can make the congregant vulnerable and dependent.

6. *Trust in the sanctuary:* Congregations are considered sanctuaries—safe places—where normal attentiveness to self-protection is not considered neces-sary. Because of this perceived sanctuary, congregants share life experiences and private information with religious leaders that they would not share with others.

Prevention Strategies

The project proposes four strategies for lowering the incidence of CSM:

1. Educate the public about CSM as "misconduct" and "abuse of power," not a consensual affair between persons of equal power. Give the public language and permission to identify what they experience as inappropriate conduct and important early warnings that can enable prevention or early intervention.

2. Provide religious education based on the scriptures about the role of power, and its use and abuse, in the workplace, the community of faith, and the family. Power and its use and abuse are not unique to religious congregations. Supervisors, teachers, community leaders, and parents need to understand and handle power appropriately, according to their religious faith. *(Study series from Baylor School of Social Work on Christianity and the Abuse of Power is forthcoming.)*

3. Provide a code of ethics and clear role expectations for leaders that protect them from multiple and conflicting roles and provide them with appropriate oversight and support.

4. Provide model legal legislation that defines sexual contact with congregants as illegal, not just immoral. See Helge and Toben, "Sexual Misconduct of Clergypersons with Congregants or Parishioners—Civil and Criminal Liabilities and Responsibilities." Visit the study web site at http://www.baylor.edu/clergy-sexualmisconduct/ to obtain that document.

4

Exploitation, Not "Affair"

Margaret Kennedy

This chapter sets the context of my study of clergy sexual abuse in the UK and Ireland and how I came to undertake it. It became increasingly apparent that child protection in churches was making some headway but protection of adults was not. Various scandals both here and in America were being dismissed as "affairs" and women not considered victims.

A Journey of Understanding

The focus of my study of clergy sexual exploitation of adult women emerged out of a journey of many years, a personal and professional discovery and experience of myself as a woman, as a professional child protection trainer and consultant, as a Christian woman (Catholic), as a feminist, as a disabled woman, as a child sexual abuse survivor and as a survivor of clergy sexual violation as an adult. It is important that I locate myself firmly as a survivor and feminist in this research. The 'personal' of my life has been political in my work; here too, the 'personal' must be integral to academic research as a feminist researcher. There is a very large part of me which adamantly refuses now to be silenced, stigmatised, or patronised by my own experience of sexual violation. This was not always the case.

After my experience of a series of severe sexual assaults at the hands of an Anglican college chaplain whilst a young student, I felt shame and never dared to speak for fear I would be judged. I knew what was happening was sexual, but I could not frame it within a discourse of 'violation' until much later. I did not know women were (and still are) "trained to be ashamed of themselves if they become victims of sexual violence" (Schüssler Fiorenza and Copeland, 1994, 31).

Later in my professional work on child abuse I came to understand the 'silencing' as a patriarchal device. We were never to speak. This for me could not be sustained as I explored female oppression and became more active and forthright in child protection within a feminist framework. Not only was I exploring a professional feminist perspective on male violence against women and children, I was also engaged in feminist theology and belonged to feminist Christian groups. The forces that silenced sexually abused children and women, as well as the forced silence of women in the church became apparent.

Naming the Violation

At the beginning of this journey, I was working as a professional with a marginalized and silenced group, abused disabled children. Many could not (apparently) speak due to speech and language difficulties or learning difficulties. However, these children did 'speak' in many different ways; but due to their disempowerment and low status, or the different ways they tried to 'tell,' they were neither heard nor heeded in any way. Paradoxically these 'voiceless' children helped me find my own voice. They showed me that their low status, created by society, leads to disempowerment, vulnerability, with their experiences ignored. I saw parallels between my experience and the experience of sexually abused disabled children, and the exploited women I was supporting in the churches.

My first way of 'speaking' was by founding a group called MACSAS— "Minister and clergy sexual abuse survivors," for women and men who were sexually abused as children or as adults by (largely) male clergy. As survivors contacted MACSAS, it became clear that Christian churches were failing one group and we needed to address the sexual violation of women as adults by clergy and ministers.

It is a powerful "common sense" discourse that priest and congregant are equal and any sexual contacts that may arise are 'affairs' (even if the clergy is celibate). But women who are part of a congregation, or seeking help, are in a subordinate position where the clergy person holds considerable power, status, education and respect. These clergy are pastorally and spiritually responsible for the care of their congregants. The clergy person, who is supposed to be 'God's representative' in this world, has an additional spiritual power over women apparently conferred by God. Feminist theologians argue that because we call God our Father we perceive also the priest as both God and Father.

Accounts from MACSAS survivors revealed that sexually abused/exploited women were dismissed. Clergy sexual exploitation/sexual abuse of adult women is hidden and ignored in all Christian denominations, yet authors testify that the most common cases within churches are exploitation of adult women in the pastoral relationships.

Women were asked to ignore what had happened, were given various explanations such as "It was an affair," "He was stressed out, it didn't mean anything," or "It's not abuse; you are an adult." Being an adult woman seemed to be an indicator of consent, so it was not seen as so serious and it was therefore not a sexual violation. It was almost universally the case that male clerics, both the offender and his superiors within the power structures of the specific Christian churches defined what had occurred.

My work shows that the 'naming' of women's violation is vitally important. Sexual assault, rape, touching, groping, intercourse with a clergy professional in his role as pastor of a women seeking his help is not an "affair." I consider sexual exploitation of women in a pastoral setting as a form of violence/violation. Over the years definitions concerning this exploitation have been deficient. The definition used in my study adds additional elements to be considered:

> Sexual violation/violence occurs when a person in authority, in role, as clergy, Minister, or Pastor uses/exploits female parishioners or those who seek his help for his own sexual gratification. This is the case whether or not women allegedly consented, since she was a 'client' or parishioner. The Pastor uses power and role to manipulate or coerce this 'consent' by various deceptions. Consent is therefore not valid within a setting where the woman seeks the advice, counsel, teaching or spiritual direction of her Pastor. Sexual violation/exploitation is the control of a woman, her mind, body and soul for reasons of sex, power, money, comfort, or affirmation without her true informed consent and obtaining these gains by various deceptive, manipulative and coercive mechanisms.

My research is my second way of "speaking" and the contribution of this thesis enables female clergy sexual abuse survivors to define "what counts" and to create a climate in churches in which the testimony and experience of women are accorded credibility and importance. The churches need empirical evidence that there is a problem and we could try together to map out these violations.

Enabling women to make their experience visible means that they have defined what counts and will be heard. They convey to all what they want to happen now, and challenge the churches in this research to take seriously their sexual violation and argue for *metanoia*—conversion, a change of heart and attitude by those churches. They ask for justice in policies and procedures, in pastoral care and recognition of all they have gone through.

Setting the Context

Professionals abusing their patients/clients through sexual "relationships" have been recognized since the early 1990s in the UK, though clergy victims were not included. Only if the clergy person was a psychologist and the women were his patients would there be recourse by her for some action.

Jenny Fasal in the 1980s identified that MIND [a mental heath organization] was aware of the problems, but there were no support structures in place for victims. Together with the late Mary Edwardes she founded POPAN in 1998—Prevention of Professional Abuse Network, later known as Witness against Abuse.

Research began within the field of therapy. The first literature on the issues in the UK was Janice Russell's *Out of Bounds—Sexual Exploitation in Counseling and Therapy* (1993).Tanya Garrett, a psychologist, conducted an anonymous survey of members of the Division of Clinical Psychology (DCP) of the British Psychological Society in relation to their experience of sexual contact with patients, and this was published in 1998. In 1994, Derek Jehu's book *Patients as Victims—Sexual Abuse in Psychotherapy and Counselling* was published. This was an overview of the issues taken from already established American literature on the subject.

Breaking Silence—Influence of American Clergy Scandals

Work in the UK on professional abuse has been minimal in stark contrast to the work in North America, where not only did the debate concerning professionals who have sex with their clients begin in the 1960s but it has been a criminal offence in many states for some years, with Wisconsin being the first state to legislate in 1984. Currently it is a crime in at least 23 states for a therapist to have sex with a client, and 17 include clergy in that group, if they are providing therapy. Two states, Minnesota and Texas are tougher still, holding clergy criminally liable even if they are providing spiritual advice and comfort.

In the early 1990s sexual abuse of children by clergy, particularly Catholic clergy, emerged through survivor testimony. Silence and the secrecy were broken and conferences with survivors speaking out were convened.

Advocacy and campaigning work to support people sexually abused as adults by clergy began.Women challenged the notion that sexual violation by clergy was only a 'child' and 'age related' crime.

International Cases of Exploitation of Women by Clergy

Cases of sexual exploitation of women by clergy are now known in many countries and across all religious groups. However, Catholic clergy remain prominent in the media. Exposure is rarely focused on the misconduct but highlights the hypocrisy of celibacy and is often used to support the argument to allow the clergy to marry.

The predominant discourse of "affairs/love" is evident both in media reports and more in-depth commentaries. Catholic priests' involvement with women is usually framed as 'love.' On close inspection some of these 'women' were under 18 and several 'love' situations were within the pastoral professional relationship.

Peter Hebblethwaite *(National Catholic Reporter,* 1996) wrote about Clelia Podesta marrying an Argentinean bishop and her book *Mi nombre es Clelia*, which caused a scandal. The relationship might have continued in secrecy had not Podesta been called to Rome and made to sign his resignation.

The Discourse of Love

The discussion below addresses the known cases within the UK and Ireland and brings the issues into focus in these isles. This indicates the exploitation of women is also part of the fabric of some clergy's lives here. It looks closely at the developments of the cases that have reached public knowledge.

In England, Chris Brain, a cleric within the Anglican Church, was found to be a prolific abuser of up to 40 women in his 'alternative' but still Anglican, Nine O'Clock Service in Sheffield *(The Independent,* 24th August 1995). The Anglican Church tried to distance itself from the activities of Chris Brain by arguing that his church was a 'cult,' suggesting Brain was a 'maverick,' even though, up until the disclosures of sexual exploitation, they fully supported his work. Chris Brain was defrocked and he left Britain. None of these 40 alleged cases reached civil or criminal proceedings for sexual assault.

Despite numerous high-profile cases, women are still perceived as willing partners. In 1996, Bishop Roddy Wright (Scotland, now deceased) fathered a child with a woman he was pastorally helping; this was seen as an 'affair,' not sexual exploitation.

Eamonn Casey, Bishop of Galway, Ireland, also fathered a child with Annie Murphy, a woman he was pastorally responsible for; this too, was seen as a love "affair." Murphy (1993) wrote about this "affair" as a 'love' story, though Casey himself frames his sexual activity as 'therapy' for Annie. Broderick (1992) in a critical analysis of Casey's life in *Fall from Grace,* (1992) presents Casey as a selfish, self-centered man. "He wanted to be a groom at every wedding and a corpse at every funeral" (120). His treatment of Annie when she disclosed her pregnancy was vicious.

Father Pat Buckley was one of the first to discuss clergy sexual misconduct in Ireland, but due to his rather unorthodox approach he is largely discounted. He put the Casey 'affair' firmly in the breach of trust category (161). In his book *A Thorn in Their Sides* (1994), he devotes a chapter to the sexual exploitation of Irish women by Catholic clergy. Therein he includes case studies of four women: Mairead, who went to her priest to discuss her inability to have a child; Deirdre, who was depressed and went for counselling to her priest, only to discover that the priest was engaging both her and a nun in a sexual relationship; Fiona, who met the priest following the death of her husband as he was helping her with the funeral; and Jan, who was married to an alcoholic and violent man and started to receive visits from a priest. He writes of one priest who exploited six women simultaneously. All these women he declared exploited.

Following publication of his views on the Casey 'scandal,' 57 women in similar circumstances wrote to Buckley. He says, "In all the cases it was the priest who initiated the relationship. It often happened when the woman went to the priest to discuss a personal or a marriage problem (Buckley, 1994,153).

In Ireland Michael Cleary, a popular 'folk singing priest,' fathered two children with Phyllis Hamilton (his 'housekeeper'). Hamilton had spent her teenage years as a patient in a psychiatric hospital following severe child sexual abuse. At 17 years old she visited Cleary for confession (she was still under the care of the hospital and lived there). Cleary, considerably older, 'persuaded' her they could be secretly married. Both Hamilton (1995) and Murphy (1993) had (male) journalists co-write autobiographies of their stories, and the "affair" discourse is used throughout.

In the UK Jenkins (1995) compiled a book of women's stories of 'love' with Catholic priests. The title *A Passion for Priests* suggests women themselves target priests. The subtitle *Women Talk of Their Love for Roman Catholic Priests,* indicates the substance of the book. She calls the relationships "affairs" but critiques the position in her introduction and conclusion. Jenkins acknowledges the exploitation by noting in the introduction that clergy who are counseling women betray women's trust, and she highlights the absence of any institutionalised ethical body overseeing these priest/counsellors. There is no official code of conduct or complaints procedures. The men are protected by the illusion that Catholic priests don't have sex and [by] their collar (19). She is scathing about Catholic Clergy who abandon women:

> Some men would say if the relationship makes them better priests, more understanding of the complexities of human emotions, more sympathetic to confusion and suffering, they are not prepared to give it up. It sounds compassionate to talk of men 'rediscovering their vocations' after having an affair. What thanks do the women receive for helping their partners to a renewal which can only benefit an entire Church? What sympathy when the man deserts them? He may return strengthened by his vows, his training, his sense of vocation. She by definition has none of this.... The men have a rescue structure built into their vocation. The women do not. (Jenkins, 1995, p274, 276)

The effect of the powerful 'love' discourse in both the Catholic Church and Anglican Church is that all priest-women relationships are now seen as loving and consenting, meaning those who are exploited have no voice. This relies on the assumption women are always willing in these relationships. There is a growing belief that such sexual relationships are condoned by church leaderships in order to keep priests in ministry, particularly if the clergy are discreet and avoid 'scandal.' There is some anecdotal evidence that bishops, too, are sexually involved with women as women share with me the local diocesan rumours.

Called to Account

This section highlights that whilst it is not entirely impossible to call clergy to account, both legally and canonically (that is, through church law) the sanctions tend to be minimal.

Fr. Frank Goodall, a Redemptorist priest (UK) was found guilty at a church tribunal in 1996 of sexually exploiting Evonne Maes, a religious Sister. Despite this, there were no sanctions against him and he continued in ministry up until his death. Maes wrote her memoir (Maes with Slunder, 1999) after leaving her convent and the church. However, women telling their own stories publicly is unusual in the UK or Ireland.

A Catholic priest, Fr. Terrance Fitzpatrick, was ordered in 2001 to pay his female victim £70,000 compensation after he was convicted of assault in the civil courts. His order, the Benedictines, said he had taken a vow of poverty and they as an Order were not allowed to use their own funds under charitable regulations. He remains in ministry.

Clergy being jailed for sexual assault is not a common occurrence; it can be argued that the discourse of 'affair' and women being 'adult,' with confusion about 'consent,' conspires against prosecutions. However, Fr. James Deadman, a Cistercian priest in Leicester, was jailed in 2001 for six years on eleven counts of sexual assault of women who went to him for help. In 2004 an Evangelical black pastor, Douglas Goodman, was jailed for sexually assaulting young women in his church in London. In 1997 a woman spoke at a conference about her rape by a priest by whom she became pregnant. He was jailed for six years (*The Guardian,* 18/9/97). An Anglican clergyman was jailed for abusing children in 2003, but he targeted and exploited their mother for access to the children. In Wales a Catholic priest was also jailed for molesting children, but it is known he also sexually molested women, though this 'remains on file.'

Cases of Anglican clergy called to account, albeit under 'adultery' charges, are reported in the media. The Anglican Consistory court presses charges under church legislation of 'conduct unbecoming' of the ministry. Whilst the Dean of Lincoln, Brandon Jackson, famously won his case in 1995, being found 'not guilty,' some clergy have lost their positions, whilst others are simply moved to another parish. Clergy are removed (un-frocked) mostly for 'adulterous' behaviour, or bringing scandal on the church. Geoff Howard (1994), Gareth Miller (1994), Keith Haydon (1999), Peter Davey (2000), Simon Oberst (2004), and Robert Graham (2004) all resigned as a consequence of 'affairs' with parishioners. The Dean of Ripon, John Methuen, faced two charges in 2005 of 'inappropriate conduct' with women but 'resigned' before the consistory court convened. Most recently Rev. David King was suspended for four years from ministry for an 'adulterous affair' with a woman who sought counselling from him (*The Times,* 12/03/ 2008).

In the UK there is confusion by both church and state about the charge to be brought, whether this should be regarded as adultery, conduct unbecoming the ministry, sexual exploitation of women, or whether clergy should be charged with assaults, rape, or other sexual offences.

Developments in the United Kingdom and Ireland

It is important also to look at the history of the sexual abuse of children and of women in the UK and Irish churches. Denominations other than Catholic largely escape media scrutiny, and it is the media who have shaped the discourse thus far. The Catholic Church proves interesting to media because of celibacy, the Anglican Church because it is the established church and the discourse of "affairs" is attractive to journalists. Most evidence comes from Anglican/Catholic accounts.

One of the possible reasons why the UK has lagged so far behind America with regards to accountability for clergy sexual exploitation is that religion has, until recently, not been a key player in mainstream public policy. Churches are smaller and the voices of women who may be sexually exploited are silenced in a largely secular culture. This is worthy of reflection since the lack of concern on a societal level is hindering progress on safety for women in churches. If compared with Ireland, a country hugely (until now) connected to Catholicism; there the betrayal of church hierarchy and priests who abuse children is front-page news with much outrage. However, it remains the case that in Ireland clergy indulging in relationships with women would generate front-page news only as 'scandal' of an affair with discussion about the inhumanity of celibacy. In the UK, these issues are not seen as worthy of reflection by the media except for high-profile cases.

In 2000, survivors from CSSA (Christian Survivors of Sexual Abuse) gave evidence to the Catholic Church's review of child protection, the Nolan Review. They recommended that because of increasing contacts from those sexually abused as adults, Nolan should include clergy sexual abuse of adult women.

Nolan did ultimately address vulnerable adults but other than mentioning learning disabled adults, failed to respond to the call for guidance CSSA sought or a clear definition:

> We have received several comments suggesting that our work might be extended to cover the arrangements the Church should make to protect vulnerable adults, such as those with learning disabilities. . . . Such an extension would go beyond our remit and our expertise. We do, however, commend the church to consider the need for policies and arrangements in this area. (Nolan Review, 2000, 2.2.1)

Unfortunately the Catholic Office for the Protection of Children and Vulnerable Adults (COPCA) uses a narrow definition of 'vulnerable adults' as set out in *No Secrets* (Department of Health & Home Office, 2000): "A person who is, or may be, in need of community care services by reason of mental or other disability, age or illness; and who is or may be unable to take care of him or herself, or unable to protect him or herself against 'significant harm' or 'exploitation.'" Women in crises, such as domestic violence, who seek the help of a clergyperson and are subsequently sexually exploited would not fall into this definition of 'vulnerable.'

A group, called 7-116 (UK) unintentionally compounds the confusion between 'exploitation' and' consenting' involvement as they define themselves as women voluntarily in secret relationships with Catholic priests. Their concern is the unfairness of celibacy for catholic priests. Whilst they argue both priests and women are being abused by the church's rule on celibacy, they do recognise exploitation:

> In the many stories we have heard it is the man in almost every case who has
> made the initial advance, encouraged the relationship and then backed away
> when faced with the implications of providing ongoing love and support to
> another person. He receives protection and often sympathy and support,
> while the woman is left bereaved and unsupported. There are other relation-
> ships which are abusive and are often the result of women having sought
> counselling help at a time when they were vulnerable. Their vulnerability is
> taken advantage of (Network, December 1996, 15).

It should be noted that churches of all denominations are at least attempting to produce ethical guidance for their clergy, albeit sometimes using the
love/affair discourse or discourse of 'harassment.' Concern is generated and
debates take place on a survivor individual/micro level and are discussed, but
Christian churches have not addressed the macro/societal level. Certainly the
public are unaware of the reality of sexual exploitation of adults by professionals generally and more so by clergy. It is urgent that more public exposure of
these issues is encouraged

Access to Knowledge

In the UK and Ireland women have had no access to knowledge about clergy
sexual misconduct against adults; very little has been written outside newspaper reporting.

In 1999 I authored/compiled *Courage to Tell,* a book of Christian women's
experience of child sexual abuse. Many women shared the negative responses of
their churches to disclosure. Churches Together in Britain and Ireland (CTBI)
wanted to advise churches on how to support survivors, and a working party was
convened to develop what came to be *Time for Action* (2002). This included a
chapter on Clergy Sexual Misconduct of Adults, the first official church docu-
mentation of this form of violation in the UK.

Ireland held its first conference on Sexual Exploitation of Women by
Professionals and Clergy, convened jointly by the Rape Crises Network of
Ireland (RCNI) and MACSAS in 2002. MACSAS held three conferences in
1998, 2004, and 2007 on clergy sexual abuse of adults in the UK.

In 1998 the UK government became concerned about vulnerable adults in
care homes, as well as abuse of adults and intimidation in courts. These concerns coalesced into government guidance, issued as *No Secrets* (2000). This was
to guide agencies on developing and implementing multi-agency policies and
procedures to protect vulnerable adults, that is, learning disabled, elderly and

mentally ill people. The 2003 Sexual Offences Act, which aimed to protect vulnerable adults, also contained specific offences that relate to breach of trust by careworkers; however, clergy are not included. Some church policies are being written with these vulnerable groups in mind. The women in this study who, in their view and mine, were sexually abused whilst vulnerable are not regarded as vulnerable or exploited by *No Secrets* or the 2003 Act. Challenging these assumptions is one strand of my work.

5

Systemic Collusion

DEE ANN MILLER

Years of studying family systems theories, coupled with years of experience in psychiatric nursing, have led me to believe that collusion is a symptom of a serious systemic thinking disorder. Therefore collusion should not be considered, as some suggest, a normal occurrence. During my time in Africa, I frequently checked the hemoglobin of African women and children, as I attempted to intervene in diseases which commonly were made much more serious because of anemia. It was rare to find a patient who was *not* anemic! But imagine how mistaken a health worker in Africa would be to conclude that anemia in African women and children is normal: "Just must be something in their genes... must be, since it is so common!"

The truth, of course, is that African women and children suffer from anemia because of other health issues. Most of these conditions will not be altered without massive changes in cultural, social, and economic systems. Doing so will require that the rest of the world change the way we think about our responsibility to stop practices that contribute to the problem.

Similarly, collusion in cases of sexual or domestic violence or in family incest is incredibly common. Yet it is not normal. Collusion, wherever it occurs, is evidence of a spiritually sick system. Yes, collusion is a systemic thinking disorder, and it has been around so long that some folks justify it by calling it normal.

As a nurse, I am trained to focus on the etiology (causes) of problems, the symptoms, and the treatment. Basic Facts about Collusion[1] offers insights into DIM (Denial, Ignorance, and Minimization) thinking and the resulting, destructive games that are highly visible in collusion. A Two-fold Treatment Approach[2] deals with treating the system. This chapter focuses only on etiology.

Individuals collude, either actively or passively, partly due to *acculturation*. In many instances, they are also *personal*. Those with a vested interest in preserving the system or the profession at any cost are much more prone to keep secrets which are deemed to be more harmful to them personally than to be helpful for the larger community. People who come from families with unresolved issues

of incest, alcoholism, drug abuse or other issues of extreme dysfunction are also
more prone to collude.[3]

Not only are we dealing with DIM thinking issues from the wider culture,
we must also consider specific ones which tend to be even more prominent in
religious communities:

Closed-system thinking—"We don't need outside help. This church or denomination can find its own answers within its own ranks, thank you."

Naiveté—When one's life revolves primarily around the activities of the clois-
tered "protection" of the institutional church, it is much easier to ignore the
realities about both the outside the world and those of the institution of which
one is so much a part. The theology of many religious communities encourages
followers to see the outside world as "evil" and those within its circle as "good."
Not seeing what is real greatly increases individual and collective vulnerability
to victimization.

Narcissism—Members of religious communities like to see themselves as
"special" children of God. This sense of being exceptional makes it easy to justify
collusion for many people.

Patriarchal thinking—Patriarchy, according to Joan Chittister, O.S.B., is
"elitism without merit." Not only does it enhance the god-image of religious
leaders, making them exempt from accountability in the warped world of collusion. It also demonizes anyone who would call their behaviors into question.
Finally, it provides help from the larger culture in giving preferential treatment
to men, a problem which is even more magnified within religious circles.

Competency issues—There appears to be a sense of hopelessness and confusion
in this area. Does the religious community have the same responsibility for setting universal standards for its professionals and volunteers? Should there be a
code of ethics? If so, how can it be effective with the divisions and factions that
exist within the community of faith? If not, who is going to protect the public
when churches are largely exempt from outside regulations? The historic "honor
system" has obviously resulted in a lot of dishonor to all concerned. If competency does not become a greater concern, how can we hope for the religious
community to hold onto any respect at all? These are difficult questions to raise.
Yet we dare not avoid them.

The "Family of God" concept—If we think of the church as a family, we are far
more prone to give solace to deviants within the group.

With my earliest roots planted in conservative religious circles in the South,
coupled with the feedback I've gotten from my writing in the past few years,
I am convinced that clergy sexual abuse, clergy domestic violence, and incest

(both in clergy and non-clergy households) is considerably more common in conservative groups than in mainline ones. There also seems to be a greater degree of physical violence involved in offenses and a greater likelihood that victims will be minors.

Perpetrators are very shrewd in seeking out systems and localities where they feel they can keep their secrets from being exposed. So conservative theology, where even healthy discussions about sexuality are extremely rare, offers some of the "safest" places for perpetrators to operate. The more rigid the rules, whether those rules are made by the Vatican or by people who insist on the automatic gospel truth attributed to every "jot and tittle" in the Bible, the more likely will be the resistance to facing the truth when it is close to home. In sum:

The degree of collusion in an institution will significantly increase in direct proportion to the evidence of the above issues within its belief system. Having lived in the worlds of both mainline and conservative Christian denominations, I find the degree of the above factors to be strikingly greater among the latter.

Clergy sexual and domestic violence within conservative circles is still largely hidden in conservative and Southern regions of the United States because of the greater degree of oppression of victims. The degree of outright persecution and marginalization of messengers in these circles, where the above characteristics are especially pronounced, seems to be even stronger than in mainline circles.

Despite recent high-profile cases, such as those in Dallas, victims from the conservative South are far less likely to report their abuses, to go public, or even to connect with other survivors. However, thanks to the Web's ability to break the isolation of survivors, this seems to be changing rapidly!

I believe the problems of collusion in conservative congregations are compounded further for several reasons:

Even large denominations, such as the Southern Baptist Convention, can hide with a lot of safety behind the "autonomous church" defense. This means that local churches in these systems are entirely responsible for hiring, firing, and supervising their employees. Yet getting into the ranks of clergy is much easier than in hierarchal systems.

There is far less exposure of clergy abuse in conservative circles than in mainline, where increasingly clergy are being required to attend workshops in order for the denomination to keep its insurance. Denominational publications which are more commonly read by laity appear much less likely to expose the issues in conservative circles.

It is commonly believed among many mental health professionals that familial incest is more common in conservative homes, where the concept of father being "the head of the house" is easily taken to this extreme. Why should this *not* be true in the institutional church as well?

Few conservative churches have policies and procedures for handling allegations. If an institution has not been able to even consider the possibility of a case by acknowledging and preparing for it in advance, victims are far more likely to remain isolated, feeling that they are either the only victim within a church or denomination or have found the only clergy offender within its ranks.

Of course, these observations apply beyond the Southern Baptist Convention. The Roman Catholic Church, for example, which has received by far the most media exposure of clergy sexual abuse, is just as conservative in its theology as Southern U.S. fundamentalism is.

6

The Sacred Trust of Ministry

Darryl W. Stephens

Case Studies

Jerome, a single man in his late 20s, is in his third year as pastor of Grace Church, a growing congregation in a bustling suburb of a major city. Marjorie, a single woman in her mid-20s, joined Grace Church two years ago after a difficult divorce. Recently, she's begun to pay more and more attention to her pastor. It is clear to others in the congregation that they have a mutual attraction to each other, and some members gossip about how they might encourage this budding romance. Eventually, Jerome asks Marjorie on a date so that the two of them can get to know each other in a more personal way. Soon they are dating regularly. Jerome chooses to keep things quiet and not to involve the church leadership in his personal affairs...

Sandra is a vivacious and dynamic lay leader at First Church. She is 34, married, and has two preschool age children. This is her fourth year in ministry with the congregation's youth group, and Sandra has developed very close relationships with many of the youth. The parents at First Church are pleased that the youth group is growing under her leadership and they appreciate Sandra's willingness to be available to her youth-group members any time of day or night via telephone, text, or email, and many youth do confide in her and call her at "odd hours" about their personal problems. Sandra is also very affectionate with the boys, especially, often greeting them with a full-body hug and kiss whenever they meet, to make them feel loved, she explains. In the church youth lounge, she is often found sitting on the sofa next to one or more of the youth, holding hands or giving backrubs. The youth consider her to be a friend...

Donald is a dynamic and charismatic senior pastor of Church of the Magdalene, a large, urban congregation. During the past five years of his 15-year ministry at Magdalene, three laywomen in his congregation—Nancy, Carol, and Johanna— have gone to the bishop with accusations that Donald has acted inappropriately with them. Each woman independently tells the bishop that Donald repeatedly groped, kissed, and fondled her in the church office. When confronted by the bishop, Donald defends himself, claiming that ladies in the church are often attracted to him, that this is not the first time he has been accused by jealous women unable to lure him from his wife, and that his award-winning record of evangelism for the past 25 years speaks for itself.

The bishop feels that her hands are tied, since Donald will neither confirm nor deny the allegations and none of the women is willing to sign an official complaint out of fear of reprisal. In fact, Donald has done the things the women accuse him of, but he thinks that he is entitled to sexual favors since he "sacrifices so much" for the church.

Each of the above cases studies depicts a leader who violated the trust of ministry through sexual behavior with a congregant. Donald is a sexual predator. He feels entitled to sex from his female parishioners and he evades responsibility for his actions when confronted by the bishop. It is easy to understand his behavior as unethical and to see the wrong in his actions. Jerome, on the other hand, is not a predator. In fact, some people may have difficulty understanding his actions as misconduct at all, since his parishioners are encouraging him and Marjorie to date. The case of Sandra depicts a ministerial leader whose lack of clearly defined interpersonal boundaries creates emotional confusion and puts herself and the youth in her care at risk. She may be a wanderer or a predator. We cannot tell from this short description. All of these ministerial leaders put the needs of self ahead of the needs of those whom they serve.

Definitions

The sacred trust of ministry is protected by ethical attention to the concepts of fiduciary duty, power, interpersonal boundaries, and consent. "Sacred trust" refers to a fundamental ethical obligation of the ministerial leader. All Christians are called through baptism to ministry. The gift of ministry comes from God. The task of ministry is entrusted to individuals. Some Christians are called by God and confirmed by the faith community as having the gifts and graces for representative ministry. Ministerial leaders may be lay or ordained and serve in countless roles, such as church school teachers, bus drivers, musicians, and preachers. These roles of leadership indicate the trust of a faith community and obligate the persons in those roles to uphold this trust. The sacred trust of ministry demands, at a minimum, that ministerial leaders will act in the best interests of those whom they serve.

"Fiduciary duty" is the legal term describing this professional obligation not to exploit others to our own advantage. Ministry, along with all other helping professions, shares this duty. Doctors, lawyers, social workers, teachers, law-enforcement officers—each of these professions accepts a responsibility to promote the best interests of others rather than self. Misconduct of a sexual nature is never simply an "affair," rather, it is a violation of the power and authority of the professional role. A lawyer, for instance, has a duty to act in the best interests of her client and to refrain from using that relationship to personal advantage. In the medical profession, the obligation to "do no harm" is expressed in the classic formulation of the Hippocratic Oath. For clergy and others in ministerial roles, this duty emerges from two thousand years of theological tradition.

The Holy Bible is replete with messages about justice and faithful ministry. The predominant theme of justice in the Hebrew Bible is protection of the vulnerable, those without power.[1] King David exemplified the leader who misuses power for personal gratification. When Nathan said to David, "You are the man!" (NRSV, 2 Samuel 12:7), he voiced God's judgment on David's misuse of his office to exploit Bathsheba and her husband. Ezekiel brought sharp condemnation on so-called shepherds who would prey on their own flock: "You have not strengthened the weak, you have not healed the sick, you have not bound up the injured, you have not brought back the strayed, you have not sought the lost, but with force and harshness you have ruled them" (2 Samuel 34:4).

In the New Testament, Jesus warns, "just as you did [not] do it to one of the least of these, you did [not] do it to me" (Matthew 25:40, 45), implying that our behavior in ministry to others is a reflection of how we would treat Jesus himself. Paul counsels those in ministry: "Do not seek your own advantage, but that of the other" (1 Corinthians 10:24). In the United Methodist liturgy of baptism, the community of faith pledges to "live according to the example of Christ" and to "surround these persons with a community of love and forgiveness, that they may grow in their trust of God."[2] Misconduct of a sexual nature is a violation of this love and trust, taking advantage of vulnerable people, who entrust their lives and souls to the care of the church and its ministers.

Sexual misconduct is an abuse of power, a violation of professional boundaries, and an exploitation of persons incapable of genuine consent. The United Methodist Church offers these definitions:

• Sexual misconduct is a betrayal of sacred trust. It is a continuum of unwanted sexual or gender-directed behaviors by either a lay or clergy person within a ministerial relationship (paid or unpaid). It can include child abuse, adult sexual abuse, harassment, rape or sexual assault, sexualized verbal comments or visuals, unwelcome touching and advances, use of sexualized materials including pornography, stalking, sexual abuse of youth or those without capacity to consent, or misuse of the pastoral or ministerial position using sexualized conduct to take advantage of the vulnerability of another…

• Sexual abuse is a form of sexual misconduct and occurs when a person within a ministerial role of leadership (lay or clergy, pastor, educator, counselor, youth leader, or other position of leadership) engages in sexual contact or sexualized behavior with a congregant, client, employee, student, staff member, coworker, or volunteer.[3]

These definitions cover anyone in church leadership, not just clergy, and describe a spectrum of objectionable actions, including those exemplified by Jerome, Sandra, and Donald.

Abuse of Power: Donald [4]

Power and its abuse are key factors in ministerial misconduct, but many clergy are genuinely confused when discussions of professional ethics focus on the concept of power. A common response of a pastor striving to exemplify "servant leadership" is, "I don't *feel* powerful." However, power in a ministerial relationship is not dependent on how the minister feels. The power of the ministerial role is a reality we can and must learn to perceive and recognize. While age, race/ethnicity, gender, wealth, education, citizenship status, and language all contribute to the power differential between persons, when a pastor interacts with a congregant, her/his status as clergy is a primary factor in determining the relative power between them. People bring their most intimate concerns to those in ministerial leadership, trusting that they have the training, expertise, and sensitivity to understand the human condition and to speak a word of divine grace and forgiveness. In short, they are entrusted to care for people's deepest needs, hurts, desires, and hopes. This is a powerful position in which to be..

Donald is a pastor who abuses his power, taking advantage of his parishioners for his own satisfaction. He exemplifies the dangerous pastor to whom Ezekiel speaks a word of judgment. Or as Nathan might speak to him, "Donald, you are the man!" Donald feels entitled to act in the way he does toward the women in his congregation, and he leverages his evangelical effectiveness and prowess as a preacher to deflect criticism. His power derives not only from his role as pastor but also from his political influence in the conference. In this instance, he exerts his power by pressuring Nancy, Carol, and Johanna not to file a signed complaint and pressuring his bishop to let the matter drop. He is a dangerous manipulator who casts himself as the victim, claiming to be the "vulnerable" party.

The term "vulnerability" refers to a relative lack of power and resources.[5] As with power, vulnerability is not dependent on the way someone feels. Clergy may feel "vulnerable" when striving to model sensitivity, openness, or servant leadership, but this feeling does not indicate a lack of power. To the contrary, many clergy are empowered to display a great degree of emotional and spiritual openness with their congregation precisely because of their role and the institutional resources available to them. Having a lot to lose is an indication of power, not powerlessness. In Donald's case, he has a 25-year career, a large-steeple pulpit, and a public image at stake (in addition to his marriage and family life). To protect himself and his personal interests, he spuriously claims to be vulnerable while leveraging tremendous institutional resources to have his way.

This is not to say that clergy can never be the victims of harassment and abuse. Young women clergy, in particular, can be vulnerable to harassment and abuse by male laypersons, especially those whose age, race, wealth, and other social factors provide them with a relatively more powerful position. Nevertheless, the person in the ministerial role is always responsible for maintaining appropriate professional boundaries.

Inappropriate Boundaries: Sandra

Interpersonal boundaries appropriately delimit the ministerial relationship. When a clergyperson interacts with a person in her congregation, she represents more than herself. She represents the congregation, the institutional church, the profession of ministry, and even God. When she dons the "collar" (either literally or figuratively), she functions in a public role with public expectations. She does not act on her own behalf. This is true whether leading public worship or providing one-to-one spiritual guidance. This is also true of laity in ministerial roles of leadership: choir directors, church school teachers, and adult volunteers with the youth group all occupy a ministerial role. Observing and honoring interpersonal boundaries allow ministerial leaders to uphold the covenant of expectation placed upon that role. The sacred trust of ministry is built on the assurance of limits.

Professional relationships differ from personal relationships in their degree of reciprocity. Ministerial relationships are asymmetrical: the pastor is there to serve the needs of the parishioner (fiduciary duty), not the other way around. The pastor is expected to provide certain services, to have professional training and expertise and to be institutionally accountable for carrying out her duties. The pastor is expected to satisfy her own needs outside of the pastoral relationship. Personal relationships, on the other hand, are mutual and less well defined. Friendships are built on the expectation of being there for each other. The mutuality of friendship means personal sharing back and forth and support of each other. Sexual intimacy, for example, should be characterized by mutuality and reciprocity. This is not true of the relationship between pastor and parishioner.

Appropriate boundaries within ministerial relationships depend on culture and context to some degree. They are not rigid rules but must be adapted and examined again and again. Different cultures have distinct expectations for appropriate physical and emotional boundaries. Even the most basic interactions, such as a conversation between two people in a public place, are governed by many tacit rules of interaction. Anyone who's ever talked to a person from a culture with a smaller radius of personal space knows the uncomfortable feeling of an interpersonal boundary being violated. In some cultures, it is customary to stand very close to the other person while talking. This disconcerting proximity causes me to take a step backward to re-establish the space to which I am accustomed. My interlocutor then steps forward to re-establish his usual interpersonal distance. This difference must be constantly negotiated as our conversation continues. Boundaries in ministry are similarly culturally defined, to some degree, and must be negotiated and re-negotiated within our faith communities.

If boundaries are somewhat flexible and context dependent, what then can we say about what is appropriate or inappropriate? Several moral tests can guide us. First, the bullhorn test: how would my actions as a ministerial leader be perceived if they were made public? This might also be called a test of transparency. A second question is: Whose needs are being met? This is the test of fiduciary duty. Are my actions as a ministerial leader in the best interests of the congregant? Or am I attempting to have my own, personal needs met through this relationship? A third question is: What ministerial service am I providing? Providing emotional and spiritual support during difficult times is a genuine function of ministry. On the other hand, sexual intimacy is not a service of the profession of ministry! A fourth test is collegial accountability and supervision. How do my supervisor and colleagues respond when I report my behavior as a ministerial leader? (Note: If I am unwilling to honestly depict and share my behavior to them, I have failed the bullhorn test, above.) Fifth, who is put at risk by my actions? This is the "do no harm" test. Sixth, how might my behavior be misperceived? This is the test of staying above reproach; avoiding the appearance of impropriety. Seventh, how important or indispensible do I feel in this relationship? Do I feel that I am the only person who can attend to these spiritual needs? Or am I just filling a role in this person's life at this time?

Effective ministry is not about me as a clergyperson. The feeling of being personally needed by others is a powerful form of dependency, and it can go in both directions. Eighth, does the person being ministered to exhibit signs of emotional dependence on the minister? (This is the companion to guideline seven.) Ninth, what kind of precedent am I setting? This is about the culture of ministry in a particular congregation. I am not a sexual predator; I know that when alone with a congregant, I will not intentionally take sexual advantage of that person. However, if I create a congregational culture that routinely accepts ministerial behavior that could put others at risk, then I set a precedent that enables a future predator easy access to vulnerable parishioners. Tenth, am I being seduced by the feeling of "exception"? Do I feel that somehow this ministerial relationship is an exception to the usual rules and limits? If I think that this relationship is different, unique, or special in a way that allows me to justify crossing the usual boundaries, I am at risk of self-deception. If I think that these guidelines don't apply in my situation, I am at great risk of misconduct. My colleagues and supervisor should alert me to this danger, if I am observing guideline four, above. These guidelines are not set in stone; they do not by themselves determine if I am guilty of misconduct. However, failure to follow any of these guidelines is a red flag warning of possible boundary violations.[6]

Sandra's case raises several red flags. Her availability 24/7 by phone, email, and other technologies of communication indicates a lack of boundaries and the danger of self-importance. Sandra's actions indicate that she perceives herself as indispensable to the youth she serves. Her physical affections with the youth raise the question of her intentions. We don't know how the male youth perceive her hugs and kisses, nor do we know how others in the congregation perceive her behavior. However, a reasonable person might have cause to wonder what is going on. Sandra is behaving in ways that could be easily misperceived, if indeed her actions are innocent. She has fallen into the danger of the appearance of impropriety. Sandra is also acting in ways that indicate she may be trying to meet her own needs for intimacy, touch, and friendship through her ministerial relationships. She is not keeping the best interests of her youth primary. This is a violation of fiduciary duty. Sandra's behavior is also questionable as professional conduct. Are kisses, backrubs, and handholding legitimate services of ministry? There are certainly contexts when these actions could be an appropriate part of ministerial support, such as comforting someone in a hospital and grieving during at a funeral.,. However, Sandra uses physical intimacy as an everyday tool of ministry. Sandra may also be causing harm to others if some of the teenagers develop unhealthy emotional and physical attachments to her. Finally, Sandra's behavior is creating a congregational culture conducive to future misconduct by others. The youth and other congregants are being trained to accept as normal some very unhealthy ministerial practices. Would the congregation be as accepting of a male youth minister behaving in the same way? She has set a bad precedent for ministry. These guidelines do not prove that Sandra is guilty of sexual misconduct. However, the multiple warning signs indicate a situation that could easily lead to misconduct if it has not occurred already. Sandra is clearly guilty of violating ministerial boundaries.

Absence of Consent: Jerome

Consent is a prerequisite to acceptable sexual intimacy, but a ministerial relationship is a context in which meaningful consent by the parishioner is often impossible. Consent is not only the ability to say "yes" but also the ability to say "no." Because of the authority of the clergyperson, the disparate power between pastor and parishioner, and the vulnerability of the parishioner, sexual contact within a ministerial relationship often lacks true consent even if the parishioner seems to agree to it. When it comes to sexual intimacy, there is no meaningful consent possible between the minister and the person seeking pastoral care.[7] This type of dual relationship is incompatible with ministry and is often indicative of poor habits of self-care.

Dual relationships are common in ministry. Unlike other professions, such as psychiatrists, clergy cannot categorically avoid friendships with those they serve. Nor would clergy want to. Because pastors live and work within a community, they often have multiple relationships with the persons in their pews. The pastor might buy books at the store owned by a parishioner, the pastor's dentist might join the church and desire to be baptized, and the pastor's children might attend school taught by men and women who sing in the choir or serve as church trustees. Pastors have many different kinds of relationships with the persons in their congregations. Entering into responsible dual relationships requires intentional and often explicit negotiation of appropriate boundaries. For example, my doctor might tell me, "Rev. Stephens, I'll attend your church as long as you only ask me for medical advice during scheduled appointments in my medical office." Likewise, I would expect that Dr. Fisher would not spend time during my annual physical exam seeking pastoral advice about his personal issues. Boundaries help us respect each other's profession, time, and privacy.

Clergy often have to work harder than other professions to establish and maintain the boundaries appropriate to their dual relationships because the work of ministry is not typically confined to office hours by appointment in a designated place of ministry. When a doctor and her patient coincidentally find themselves at the same grocery store, the doctor is clearly "off duty" and would not appreciate a spontaneous request for a medical opinion. However, when a pastor is grocery shopping, this might be an integral activity necessary to effective ministry in that community. It might be an occasion to offer invitation, assurance, and spiritual support. Indeed, the challenge for clergy is how to take time off. How can clergy set aside time and opportunity to attend to their own needs?

Self-care for clergy and other ministerial leaders is vital to a healthy work/life balance and appropriate boundaries in ministry. In order to be fully present for and attend to the best interests of those they serve, ministerial leaders must also have personal time and personal relationships that allow their own needs to be met. If clergy attempted to be in ministry all of the time with everyone who enters their lives, they would do themselves and others a great disservice. They would inevitably begin using their ministerial relationships to satisfy their personal needs. Self-care for clergy means, at the least, taking a day off every week, turning off phone and email at certain times of day, and cultivating friendships with persons completely removed from their ministerial setting. Regarding their own sexual needs, clergy must recognize that they cannot be a person's lover and pastor at the same time.[8]

Jerome's case illustrates some of the complexities of dating for clergy. He and Marjorie clearly have a ministerial relationship: she joined the church under his leadership, and he has served as her pastor for two years. This relationship precedes their dating relationship chronologically and takes priority for Jerome even after their romantic liaison commences. What may appear to be a consensual relationship involving sexual intimacy between two adults is most likely not a relationship to which Marjorie is free to consent.

The guidelines above offer several red flag warnings for Jerome. Jerome fails the bullhorn test. His effort to keep their dating relationship secret is an indication of lack of transparency. There is also no evidence that he is seeking collegial support and supervision. He fails the accountability test. Jerome is also operating as if his relationship were an exception to the dangers inherent in dating a parishioner, indicating the danger of self-deception. Jerome still maintains the façade of a pastoral relationship with Marjorie even as they begin dating. Clearly, he has prioritized his own needs over the fiduciary responsibility he owes to her. Furthermore, who is being put at risk in this situation? Examining this dual relationship closely reveals that Jerome is putting Marjorie at more risk than he is willing to assume himself. If this romance encounters rocky terrain, to whom can Marjorie turn for pastoral support? Clearly she would need to turn to someone other than Jerome. Jerome's primary role in her life has changed from pastor to lover. However, it is not at all clear from Jerome's behavior that he shares this priority. Otherwise, he would be more transparent about and accountable for his actions. Marjorie has already lost a pastor, and Jerome has not helped her find a new one. The congregation is also being put at risk. When a romance goes sour, people take sides. What would happen to this congregation if this couple had a messy break-up? In many actual cases, the congregation becomes divided and community is significantly ruptured.

How could this dating scenario be improved so as to reduce the risks and increase accountability?[9] First, Jerome should acknowledge that he can't be both pastor and lover to Marjorie. If they desire an amorous relationship, one or both of them will have to find a new church. Second, transparency requires that Jerome and Marjorie be public about this dating relationship. Jerome should contact his district superintendent for guidance, and he should alert the staff-parish relations committee. Third, these parties along with some trusted colleagues should hold him accountable to his professional duties and help him establish safeguards to reduce the possibility of doing harm to others. Fourth, he will have to work carefully to avoid normalizing this behavior in the life of the congregation. If the congregation comes to accept the situation of their pastor dating a parishioner as normal, Jerome will be setting a precedent that may prove destructive to healthy ministry. If single women joining this church thought that they were being viewed as potential dating partners for the pastor, this would detrimentally affect the ability of the pastor to minister to them.

One of the most disturbing aspects of this scenario, even if these safeguards were put into place, is the likelihood that Marjorie is not really free to genuinely consent to sexual intimacy with Jerome. She joined this congregation immediately after a difficult divorce. If she has worked through her grieving of the end of this marriage, it is likely that this church and its pastor, Jerome, played a significant part in providing spiritual support. This would have increased the power imbalance already inherent in the ministerial relationship. If, on the other hand, she has not worked through her grief, she is even more vulnerable on an emotional level. The ability to genuinely consent to a sexual relationship decreases in proportion to the depth of pastoral relationship.

Myths about Misconduct

1. It is just an affair. To call it an "affair" is to focus only on the sexual relationship; but the real issues are the clergyperson's violations of the sacred trust of ministries, breach of fiduciary responsibility, violation of professional boundaries, and abuse of power.

2. They're consenting adults. They're both to blame. When there is a significant imbalance of power in a relationship (as there is between a pastor and a parishioner), it is the pastor's responsibility to maintain appropriate professional boundaries. Blaming the victim is an attempt to avoid confronting the perpetrator.

3. It's their own business. A sexual relationship is considered to be personal business. But even if both parties are single, a sexual relationship between a pastor and a parishioner affects the entire congregation, and makes it more difficult for the pastor to be a minister to the whole congregation.

4. It's best to let *them* work it out. Clergy sexual misconduct is a violation of professional ethics and is even a criminal offense in some states. It is the responsibility of the church—not the alleged victim—to hold clergy accountable to professional standards of conduct.

5. The pastor resigned. *Resignation doesn't close a case.* Closing a case prior to adjudication abrogates justice for all parties. Facts may never be investigated, innocence or guilt may never be determined, the truth may never be told. Even if the pastor resigns, it is best to complete the investigation and adjudication process.

6. Secrecy protects the church. Failure to disclose appropriate information to a congregation regarding an allegation of misconduct—and the outcome of the just-resolution process—only fuels rumors and misinformation, and denies the healing power of truth-telling. Appropriate disclosure does not mean spilling all the facts, but it does require informing people to the extent that they have a need to know about their pastoral leadership.

7. Psychological screening will eliminate misconduct. While psychological evaluations are an important parts of the screening process for ministerial candidates, this process will not eliminate the problem of future clergy misconduct in the church. The doctrine of sin reminds us of this.

8. A "zero tolerance" policy will eliminate misconduct. If a church is too quick to dismiss any clergyperson accused of any form of misconduct, a culture of secrecy may develop. Due process and the hard work of discernment about degrees of violations will contribute to justice and healing for all parties.

9. No news is good news. A church that has no reports or allegations of misconduct is not necessarily free of misconduct. In fact, effective education of clergy and laity about appropriate boundaries increases awareness of misconduct, often resulting in an increase in misconduct cases, at least in the short term.

10. A pastor can never be the victim. Clergy can be harassed and abused by parishioners just as anyone can be the victim of a crime. Churches should have a policy about how to handle complaints of lay harassment of clergy. It is still the

clergyperson's responsibility to maintain appropriate professional conduct and boundaries, however. Church should be a safe place for clergy and lay workers as well as parishioners.

Upholding the sacred trust of ministry requires leaders who are attuned to the complicated dynamics of power, interpersonal boundaries and consent within ministerial relationships. At the heart of the ethical obligation of ministry is fiduciary duty—a commitment by all persons in ministerial roles of leadership to act in the best interests of those whom they serve. Failure to observe prudent safeguards and to avoid common dangers puts many people at risk. Faithfulness to ethical standards of ministry creates safer and healthier congregational communities, enabling the church to more fully live out its call to be Christ for world.

7

Speaking Truth to Power

W. Richard Sipe

The Survivors Network of Those Abused by Priests (SNAP) has always aimed to speak truth to power. That task may be demoralizing, but truth "is always less demoralizing than the most encouraging lie."

We seem powerless against a church with its powerful connections, riches, and political resources of every kind. We gain our power by accepting our powerlessness and turning to a higher power—truth.

First, the Gospel gives us guidance.

Second, despite any pain involved, survivors must face their experience of abuse at the hands of clergy and church to garner insights about the traps and systemic power of bishops and priests who lure children into sexual assault and betrayal.

Third, what ensures the perpetuation of clergy abuse? What role can we powerless people play in protecting others from clerical sexual abuse?

One power we have is to tell the truth that exposes the myth at the vortex of the church's crisis and perpetuates abuse—that clergy are sexually safe.

Naming Abuse

In 1988 I met three people who were concerned about sexual abuse by Catholic priests: Jeanne Miller had gained some national notice when she wrote a book about her son's abuse by their pastor. She used a pen name and disguised her real identity when she appeared on national television. Despite that, she was driven from her parish, which treated her as a traitor for speaking about the abuse.

She organized a group in 1992 that sponsored the first national meeting dedicated to the concerns of victims and survivors of clergy abuse. Three hundred people attended. Among the speakers were Fr. Thomas Doyle, a canon lawyer who remains an outspoken advocate for abuse victims, and Jeff Anderson, a civil attorney who continues to lead the assault on clergy abuse throughout the world.

With their inspiration and the support of many survivors and advocates, another national meeting to discuss clergy sexual abuse assembled in 1994.

One bishop attended the meeting and wept openly when he listened to victims reporting their abuse in public. The lasting contribution of these people was to give voice to the afflicted and to encourage them to declare themselves publicly in an organized way.

Barbara Blaine and Dave Clohessy are two other people I met at the same time. Their challenge to advocacy was purchased at an even higher price. They were the immediate victims of sexual betrayal by priests. They had to fight the battle of survival and have always been primarily dedicated to the healing process, one victim at a time. They have become a clear voice for thousands.

Their power has come from that personal and individual fight for truth-telling. They have supported and inspired thousands of other victims to pool their experience, declare the truth of clergy abuse, and join the ranks of survivors. The fight for truth helps to prevent future abuse, but that battle is not easy. There is always a price to pay. The forces against truth are formidable. What are the religious forces that oppose truth? Why have religious leaders put up such daunting resistance to the reality that some clergy, who should protect children and the vulnerable, do in fact violate them?

None of the gospels say anything about the sexuality of Jesus; they do tell us that he was poor—not a place to lay his head; and that he had no worldly power—he willingly rendered to Cesar material power. He was powerless. He instructed his disciples in a lesson they would have to know well—not to fear the powerful people; to trust the power of truth, even harsh, demoralizing truth spoken by the powerless. "Fear not to speak the truth." Or: "Nothing is concealed that will not be revealed, nor secret that will not be known.... Be not afraid" (Matt 10: 26-27). Christ knew what he would have to suffer for telling the truth. It is true now, and always has been, that those who speak truth to power will suffer for it. You can be sure of that.

Truth and Religious Power

With Jesus' words in mind, reflect on what victims of clergy sexual abuse have suffered at the hands of priests, bishops, their lawyers, and accomplices in the process of cover-up, denial, delay, and deception in fighting the truth that survivors have to tell.

Systemic religious power has amassed a formidable army in opposition to the simple truth of the story that victims have to tell: some clergy are not chaste, some fail to practice the virtues they preach. The courage of survivors has forced some bishops to concede, albeit with great reluctance, the truths that the vulnerable tell: there is corruption in high places. But religious powers still have not learned to embrace the truth. They still persist in minimizing the problem of sexual violence among their ranks.

Grand jury reports conducted in the United States give victims some consolation. They all lay the blame for the sexual crisis in the Catholic Church at the doorstep of power. Bishops discouraged victims from reporting abuse, conspired to conceal abuse, failed to report possible criminal offenses to appropriate authorities, and neglected to track allegations against priests.

But the full tragedy of clergy abuse is still undefined. In 1983 11.4 percent of the priests active in the Archdiocese of Los Angeles were subsequently identified as sexual abusers. Seventy-five percent of all Los Angeles parishes had at least one abusing priest on staff and five to eight perpetrators served on the staff of several parishes. There is little evidence that bishops are listening to what documents are telling about abuse. Bishops have not listened, and are not listening to those concerned with the roots of the problem of clerical sex abuse.

Survivors of abuse have tried for decades to get religious power to listen to stories of violation and take remedial action. One concern was validation of the horrible truth of assault. Another drive is to ensure that abusers would not abuse others. Church authorities still have not heard victims. They have learned to "deal" with complaints. They have increased their public relation efforts and skills. One reporter said that bishops have become "more slick." Why is the church spending all this time, money, and energy fighting the truth and resisting what abuse survivors have to teach them?

Other victims have found the courage to come forward because of the example of survivors. Together survivors have mobilized—or rather inspired—the media to speak up, despite their own reasons to fear adverse pressure from the church. Victims have enlisted the help of courageous lawyers in the cause of prevention.

I have reviewed thousands of stories of clergy abuse. I have waded through several thousand depositions in abuse cases. I have some idea of the price that victims have to pay to tell their stories to bishops' lawyers, who insult, accuse, discredit, and demean victims, re-abusing them through the process. In all my years, I have never met a more compromised group of men and women than the lawyers working for bishops who, like Pilate, wash their hands and take no responsibility for the ordeal they put victims through. They write off pastoral concerns with, "That's what lawyers do."

The recorded testimony of some of the bishops and cardinals patently avoids truth and utilizes forgetfulness that verges on perjury. No intelligent person can miss the truth behind clergy denials and protestations of innocence and ignorance.

Some footage of a Cardinal's deposition is recorded in Amy Berg's 2006 prizewinning documentary *Deliver Us from Evil.*

Many victims of clergy abuse are subjected to harrowing examinations. Church authorities and lawyers often demand proof that borders on voyeurism. "Where, how, when did he touch you? Details. Was it on the skin? How did you feel? Did you enjoy it?" Church powers demand details and specifics far beyond what any reasonable person needs to assess the validity of an allegation.

Why? Victims of clergy violations are presumed villains. Even in apologies, bishops fail to take responsibility for the causes of abuse and their part in cover-up and preferring image to honesty. "Psychiatrists" misled them. "Lawyers" gave them bad advice. They are sorry for "suffering" and apologize generically. But church authorities fail to take direct responsibility for their part in neglect, denials, deception, and delays in coming to terms with the problem of clergy sex.

Why? Church authority still vigorously opposes the truth that victims are telling. United States bishops are spending billions of dollars to fight the truth. Why? Because they are the white-washed sepulchers of this generation. That does not mean that churches do no good. But it does mean that when power fears and resists truth, it becomes destructive.

Power and Powerlessness

Many related questions emerge from exploring the history and continued failure of bishops to deal honestly and proactively with the problem of sexual abuse. *The crisis of clergy abuse poses questions for every Christian.*

Power—fame, status, force, money—is so universally admired and sought after in society today that it is easy for a person to forget the power of powerlessness—Christ's message. Religious power confronts everyone with valid questions. Have I trusted in the power of others rather than the truth in myself? What leads a person to trust and even defend a priest who abuses? Why is it forbidden to think that a priest would be sexual and abusive? Is it because power protects even thoughts about a priest? He deserves the highest respect because he represents God. He is sexually safe. He gives up sex to serve God.

We all want the safety we think exists in the strong, rich and powerful. What part do we play in allowing the sexual crisis to come about? How does it persist, when bishops knew all along that some priests do sexually abuse vulnerable congregants? Why do bishops continue to spend your resources to deny that truth? Why do we support them?

Are we afraid of truth? Can we embrace our powerlessness, as Jesus did, neither fearing nor cowering before riches, fame, and power?

What can we learn from how bishops handled the abuse crisis? Have we played a part in secrecy, resistance, continuing denial and tolerance for abuse? Are we too eager to think the crisis is over? Do we want to return to business as usual rather than work for sexual reform? The systemic roots of clergy abuse have not been eradicated.

Reform will come not from power, but from truth.

That is the power of Christian powerlessness.

8

Clergy Sexual Abuse of Adults

Pamela Cooper-White

Katya[1] shakes her head and tears well up in her eyes as she asks, "How could I have been so stupid? How could I have been taken in by him like that?" Several years ago Katya's children were growing up, and she was a lay volunteer with her church youth group. Noticing her talent with the teenagers, the pastor, Sam, suggested that she become a member of the parish staff and worked with the church council to create a paid youth director position for Katya. She was ecstatic. All her years of experience were being validated for the first time—she was a professional now! She grew in the job, read voraciously, received more training, and considered going to graduate school for an education or psychology degree.

But all this was short-circuited. The pastor began to ask her to lunch and to spend more and more time with her discussing her work with the youth and more philosophical questions about the future of the church. Finally, one day at lunch, he sat next to her instead of across from her. With his knee brushing hers, he reached over and took her hand. "Katya," he said, "I'm going to take a big risk here. I think you're feeling some of the same feelings that I am. Am I right?" He looked into her eyes. Her own eyes filled with tears. Her husband Bob had not shown this much interest in her in years. His work kept him on the road a great deal, and although she loved him, there was not much sexual attraction. There never had been. They had dated in high school and married in college. It was what everyone had expected, and they were "in love," but Katya had never felt real sexual desire before. Now there was an attractive man, learned, gentle, sensitive—even *holy*—who was encouraging her talents, and taking her ideas seriously. He was gazing into her eyes and telling her he was in love with her. It was like a novel.

They went to her home that afternoon and touched and kissed. They didn't make love—he said it wouldn't be right since they were both married, and she felt the same way. But they began to talk freely with each other about their love and about when the timing would be right for a deeper sexual involvement.

They even saw his therapist once to talk about their growing romance. The therapist encouraged them to be honest with their spouses and to begin planning their divorces so that they could express their love more openly. Katya had grave reservations, however, because she did not want to break up her family and still loved her husband.

Finally, Katya's husband came home and announced that his company wanted to transfer them out of state. Katya agonized over what to do. She felt she could not say anything to Bob about her feelings for Sam, and although she would miss Sam terribly, she passively fell in with the plans to move. She went into a deep depression and often found herself weeping silently in church. The day the moving van arrived, Sam called and asked to see her. Her heart leaped, and she wondered if he had come up with a last-minute plan for them to be together. He came to the house while Bob was out. "I can't stay," he told her, "I just want you to know that I've told my wife everything. We never should have gotten involved, and I hope you understand that we can never see each other again. Please don't try to contact me." Katya was shattered. She moved to her new home in a fog of desperation and misery. She blamed herself for everything and wondered what she had done wrong. She abandoned her plans for graduate school and questioned whether she could even go to church again. Everything reminded her painfully of Sam, and she no longer trusted any minister.

Peg was going through a divorce. Her abusive husband had kidnapped both children in the course of a scheduled Christmas visit and took them out of state. Peg was wild with grief, desperate to get her children back, and afraid for their well-being. As she shared more and more of her feelings with her pastor, Rick, he began to hug her and hold her to comfort her.

"Come closer," he said. "You've been trying so hard to hold it all together for your kids, to be brave and strong. But you have a little girl inside of *you* that needs to be taken care of, too." Peg told me, "It is my recollection that I was working as secretary and work was done and he locked the door. He didn't ask if I wanted to make love...he said that he loved me, pulling me close, and specifically said, 'It is you who must set the boundaries in our relationship.' Being needy, gut level desiring touch, I began our physical session (after months of his touching my hair, stroking my shoulders and back, holding me). We had sex in his office. I shall never forget his comments about my setting the limits—after months of his determining I had none."

In a first draft of this chapter, I had written, misremembering, that Rick had put a blanket on the floor. Peg corrected me: "Reading your version did bring up shame. It sounded so much more romantic than it was. It's funny how your saying he put a blanket on the floor touched me. That phrase sounded so caring…as there never was a blanket."

Peg saw Rick sexually for a number of years, even agreeing to visit him when he moved hundreds of miles away. Rick swore her to secrecy, because "the parish just wouldn't understand." The secrecy wore her down, and she began to confront him about getting married. Her divorce had been finalized long ago, and her children were back with her. Why couldn't they make their relationship public? Rick became more remote and finally ended the relationship. Soon after, he married another parishioner in his new congregation. Years later, Peg finally told a women's group at her church what had happened and found out that several other women had been similarly drawn into sexual relationships with Rick when they were going through crises in their own lives.

A Long-Held Secret

Despite an increased awareness of other forms of violence against women, only a few works until recently addressed the issue of pastors' sexual abuse of adult parishioners.[2] Most writings before the 1990s framed the problem as a psychosocial one rather than placing it squarely in the spectrum of power abuse, and many, especially from a more evangelical perspective, still do. Important exceptions are Marie Fortune's *Is Nothing Sacred? When Sex Invades the Pastoral Relationship*[3] and Peter Rutter's *Sex in the Forbidden Zone: When Men in Power— Therapists, Doctors, Clergy, Teachers, and Others—Betray Women's Trust.*[4]

My own observations about this particular topic come from working since 1989 as a consultant and group facilitator for survivors of clergy exploitation. I have consulted in more than one hundred cases of clergy sexual abuse, both with victims and with denominational executives, and served as an expert witness in a number of court cases involving abuse by clergy and spiritual leaders. Through these consultations, I have witnessed the lasting devastation and anguish that these women have experienced, some for many years. Through this work, the many parallels between sexual abuse by clergy and incest and intimate partner violence have become increasingly clear to me. Such parallels are particularly apt, because the church is so often portrayed as family.

Clergy sexual abuse—defined as clergy engaging in sexual or romantic relationships with their parishioners or counselees—is much more prevalent than is commonly supposed. Some estimates even exceed the 5 to 13–percent figure ascribed to male psychotherapists.[4] Statistics from research conducted in the

1980s when clergy sexual abuse was first being uncovered indicated that somewhere from one out of eight to one out of three clergy had crossed sexual boundaries with their parishioners.[5] Of all extramarital contact self-reported by clergy in one study, over two-thirds was with a counselee, staff member, lay leader/teacher, or other congregant.[6] Thirty-one percent of clergy in the same study reported that they experienced *no* consequences for extra-marital contact, and only four percent said their churches ever found out about what they had done.[7] In the early 1990's, a PhD student at Fuller Theological Seminary surveyed 300 clergy, and found that 39 percent had had sexual contact with a parishioner, and almost 13 percent had engaged in sexual intercourse.[8] Over 76 percent of clergy in another study reported knowing of a minister who had sexual intercourse with a parishioner.[9]

More recently, even after the implementation of policies and mandated trainings on clergy sexual ethics and boundaries in over 35 denominations,[10] a review of the literature finds a range of 0.3 to 37 percent of clergy sexual abuse across denominations.[12] Most recently, a study by social scientists at Duke and Baylor Universities estimated in 2009 in a random survey of 3,559 Americans that between 2 and 4.2 percent of women who attended a congregation at least monthly were the target of a sexual advance by clergy during their adult life,[13] and 8 percent had knowledge of clergy sexual misconduct in their congregations.[14] The authors estimated that an average of 8 women in a typical 400-member congregation have experienced sexual abuse by clergy, and 32 of 400 had experienced clergy sexual misconduct occurring in their community of faith. The study also found that 92 percent of advances made toward women were made in secret, and roughlytwo-thirds of the offenders were married.[15] These are compelling figures, and there is still no indication in any research to date that any one religion or denomination is more prone to such sexual misconduct than any other.[16]

In my own survey of senior-level pastoral counselors, published in 2001, respondents estimated the prevalence of sexual misconduct in their own profession to be slightly higher than average estimates reported in the literature: an estimated mean percent of 14.5 percent (with a wide range of estimates, from 1 to 50 percent). Many respondents had heard direct reports of sexual boundary violations from both colleagues and clients: over 1/3 had heard a colleague tell them of crossing a sexual boundary with a client, 2/3 had heard a client report another therapist crossing a sexual boundary with him or her (with a mean of 2-3 incidents told with a range of 1 to 10), and 82 percent had heard a client report of a clergyperson crossing a sexual boundary with him or her (with an average of over 4 incidents told, within a range of 1 to 40). A high majority, 87 percent of pastoral counselors, had heard a client report of a clergyperson crossing a sexual boundary, with an average of over 5 incidents told.[17]

Clergy sexual abuse of adult parishioners is often seen by both fellow parishioners and by denominational executives as something else—a problem with alcohol, for example, or an emotional or relationship problem of the pastor or the parishioner, or a parish conflict. A single pastor relating intimately with a single parishioner is typically seen as an acceptable and even time-honored practice. I argue, however, that such intimate relating is always a boundary violation and that it is always the pastor's ethical responsibility to maintain appropriate boundaries.[18]

As with rape, a pastor's sexual or romantic involvement with a parishioner is not primarily a matter of sex or sexuality but of power and control. For this reason, it is, clergy sexual abuse,[19] not an "affair"[20] or a matter of private sexual activity between consenting adults. Even when adultery is involved, unfaithfulness is not the primary issue. I have found that a majority of ministers who enter into romantic or sexual relationships with parishioners do so primarily because there is an imbalance of power between them at the onset, and because they need to reinforce and heighten the intensity of that power dynamic. This need is driven by internal forces and is reinforced by societally conditioned expectations that women will function as a nurturing, sexual servant class to support men's external achievement.

As Marie Fortune has outlined in *Is Nothing Sacred?* there can be no authentic consent in a relationship with unequal power. No matter how egalitarian a pastor's style of ministry, he carries an authority as pastor that cannot be set aside. I have deliberately used the term "he" here, because my experience and that of others in the field indicate that the vast preponderance of cases involve male clergy.[21] Also, the power imbalance is much more clearly tipped by societal reinforcement in the male clergyman's direction. It is possible for a male parishioner, particularly one with special financial or organizational clout—a church council member, for example—to harass a woman minister. Such abuse also can occur between pastors and parishioners of the same sex. In such cases, power dynamics still pertain, and are further complicated by internalized homophobia and additional pressures and fears on the victim not to disclose or report.

The clergy role carries a great deal of power in and of itself, and one of the most insidious aspects of that power is the role of "man of God." In some sense the minister carries ultimate spiritual authority, particularly in the eyes of a trusting parishioner who looks to him for spiritual guidance and support. But the male minister possesses other forms of power stacked beneath it: As a man, he carries the power society confers upon men and socializes them to hold over women, often in the guise of being for their own good, as protectors. He is often physically stronger and more imposing. He may also be an employer. He may also assume a teaching or mentor role, which encourages her to listen to his advice and correction and sets her up for a particularly virulent form of psychological abuse. Often, he also functions as her counselor, with all the transference inherent in such a relationship. Parallels to incest pertain within the church "family," and can hold similar traumatic consequences for victims as in cases of intrafamilial abuse.

Because of this power, just as in the relationship between therapist and client, there needs to be a commonly accepted ethical code—yet to be established—that ministers must not ever get involved with parishioners, and must avoid as much as possible getting into the area of dual relationships.[22] This is admittedly sometimes difficult in the parish context—the minister is set up as friend, pastor, religious/spiritual advisor and pastoral counselor, administrator and CEO, and even employer for many of the same people—and at the same time is the parish's employee.[23] Nevertheless, the pastor must remain aware that dual relationships—even friendships—can all too easily become exploitative or inappropriately intimate. While dual relationships are sometimes difficult to avoid, pastors should be trained to be conscious of the potential for harm, and to understand that as clergy and as professionals they hold the ethical responsibility for keeping boundaries clear and intact. From the perspective of working with victims, I have insisted on an absolute taboo against sexual or romantic relating with parishioners, because the potential for devastating harm is too great. More will be said below about single clergy dating.

What Is the Harm Done?

Harm done to victims may be framed in terms of the opportunities ministers have for positive life-giving, healing work, and how these opportunities are destroyed by violation of sexual boundaries:

1. In our role as pastoral caregivers, we have an opportunity to heal and strengthen fractured boundaries; many parishioners are suffering from childhood abuse and bring this need. It is deeply damaging for him to initiate a sexual relationship and exploit this vulnerability for his own needs and fantasies. Even if a parishioner appears to be taking the initiative, and/or acts out sexually, the minister should recognize this as a possible cry for help. The last thing he

should do is read it as a valid invitation. In the ideal, the pastoral relationship can and should be a sacred trust, a covenantal place of safety and nurture where a parishioner can come with the deepest wounds and vulnerabilities, and even act out sexually, and through appropriate modeling of boundaries and healthy response, the pastor can begin to empower her to heal those wounds. The harm when this is exploited is no less than a violation of sacred space, which further ruptures and destroys the woman's boundaries, devastating her sense of self and her mental health. What every therapist knows (or ought to) about this should also be required training for every pastor.

Moreover, no one is without wounds. No matter how professional, how well educated, how polished in appearance, every parishioner has vulnerabilities. If the church is truly to touch our inner lives at the deepest places, then it must be a consecrated place of safety in which people can bring their fragility, their wounds, to be anointed with assurances of God's grace. In order to be truly ministered to by the church's ministers, people must feel free to bring their whole selves, including their vulnerabilities, without fear of violation, exploitation, or re-abuse.

2. In our authority role, we have an opportunity to be role models of appropriate uses of power and authority. As religious leaders, we can emphasize power-in-community, leavened with responsible power-for, rather than a power-over process model in the parish. The harm done by sexual relationships, especially as they are usually clandestine, is to reinforce a traditional male power-over dynamic, and to breed a closed, destructively hierarchical parish model. Such a parish dynamic personally reinforces the victim's socialization to lesser power and meaning, and more generally erodes the confidence and leadership of the entire congregation.

3. Through our pastoral role, we have opportunities to encourage, validate, and uplift the gifts and talents of our parishioners. When a pastor focuses on a woman's sexuality, her other gifts and competencies are devalued. Frequently the very talents that attracted him to her in the first place are gradually discounted by him once the sexual relationship begins.

4. Finally, when as pastors we violate a parishioner's boundaries, we are stealing from her the appropriate, powerful, and sustaining relationship of spiritual guidance and support that the church has represented to her. Particularly because of the threats to her own reputation, clergy sexual abuse robs her of an important arena for her creativity and contributions (although he will frequently encourage and exploit these for his own ends while he can). Countless victims report in the aftermath of this abuse that they not only lost their own

parish community, but their trust was so violated that they felt they could not go back to church anywhere.

Who Loses?

Both pastor and victim lose. Their families lose. The congregation loses. And the wider church and community loses.[24] But the woman victim loses the most and, sadly, as things still stand in most denominations, the pastor loses the least. Typically, once such a relationship or multiple relationships are uncovered, he gets a slap on the wrist and is referred to counseling, often with a great deal of sympathy. The parish is left to cope with feelings of betrayal and rage, which are often directed at the woman as seductress. The pastor's family is left to cope with their anger at his betrayal, often dealt with by minimization and denial, and blame of the parishioner. His wife is sometimes also caught in a power dynamic in their own relationship, which has her feeling confused, abused, and fearful. The family of the woman is often broken up and the burden of blame placed on her. She loses her reputation, her parish, sometimes her job, and sometimes her whole life in the community—especially in a small town or in a small community within a community.

In the past, the best she could usually expect from her denominational leaders was sympathy, but no real justice—that is, no real action taken against the pastor to prevent him from doing it again, and no real recognition of the seriousness of his violation. At worst, she could expect disbelief or blame. This is changing slowly with education, but still in the vast majority of cases, justice is at best partial.

The Case against Clergy Dating Parishioners

One of the greatest areas of resistance in the church, especially among clergy, to an absolute proscription against romantic involvement with parishioners, is the issue of single clergy dating single parishioners. Seminarians genuinely wonder if they will ever find a partner who shares their religious beliefs and practices if they cannot seek her within the parish. Veteran clergy also wonder what this means for colleagues who married parishioners, following time-honored practice—are they now to be condemned?

The decision of some regional church bodies to implement a qualified standard that permits clergy dating under some circumstances is usually motivated by a genuine and caring desire to be pastoral to clergy. In particular, the case is often cited of clergy who had married parishioners in the past, and for whom the arrangement seems to have worked out very well. Passing new codes and standards seemed judgmental toward these senior colleagues. But there is another way of approaching this issue with compassion, without judgment on such long-standing marital relationships. That is to say, many churches has and denominations have made (and in many places are still making) a paradigm shift that is difficult for many. (It is already becoming the law of the land—for example, sex with parishioners is a crime in Arkansas and Texas by virtue of the fiduciary relationship, and is criminalized in eleven more states and the District of Columbia if it occurs within a counseling context.[25]) Just as sex roles have slowly changed since the latter part of the 20th century, including our understanding of marriage as a more equal partnership, so our understanding of all professional roles has undergone revision—involving all professions, not just that of the clergy. It is not necessary or appropriate to condemn anyone who operated under the old paradigm when it worked and, importantly, when *no complaint* is being brought. But times have changed, and we need to act on what we know now about the imbalance of power in professional relationships, and the duty of the professional to safeguard ethical boundaries, especially when we turn our gaze toward policy-making and the prevention of future harm.

Because my working definition of pastor-parishioner romantic involvement is that it is not primarily about sex, but about abuse of power and misuse of the professional role, I am concerned about the growing trend in denominational policies of making allowances for single clergy dating single parishioners.[26] Ethicist Karen Lebacqz and pastor and former denominational executive Ronald G. Barton have tried to solve this dilemma by identifying a separate category of clergy, the "normal neurotic," for whom it may be difficult and fraught with dangers, but for whom it may not be ethically wrong to date certain persons in the parish who are single, mature, healthy, and not terribly vulnerable.[27] They elaborate safeguards to minimize the possibility of exploitation, in particular, not allowing the relationship to be clandestine, and finding the parishioner another pastor.

However, in my view this sidesteps the central issue of the imbalance of power and the vulnerability, by definition, of every parishioner without exception. Several points are to be considered:

1. The standard of conduct needs to be firm, so that the burden of proof for any exception needs to be on the pastor, as the professional. Otherwise, it is still up to the victim to prove that it was abuse. Many survivors say while still involved in the situation that they *are* mature, capable, and willing participants.

Often the woman's presenting issues for counseling after the relationship has ended, sometimes years later, are depression, anxiety, inability to trust or form relationships, loss of faith, or just a vague sense of "why can't I seem to get over this?"[28] Only in therapy does she come to realize that the relationship with her pastor was, in fact, exploitive. Then she has to face proving it.

No matter how apparently mutually consenting the relationship, it is important to remember that *as soon as any form of romantic relationship has begun, the parishioner has already lost that pastor as a pastor.*

2. There are also implications here for what we now know about professional self-care. I have often heard single pastors ask, "But where else will I ever meet somebody if not in my parish? I work sixty to seventy hours a week, and everyone I know, my whole social life, is with the congregation." My response to this is that we, as clergy, need to learn to limit our urge to be ever-present and ever-available, and we need to cultivate a social and personal life beyond the parish—for our own health!

3. Who is to be the arbiter of who is mature and able to enter into a relationship with a pastor, and who isn't? Who is "too vulnerable," and who isn't? Is it really enough to draw the line at whether pastoral care/counseling is officially occurring? We should all be encouraged in our faith journeys to bring our deepest wounds—which we all do have, however competent and accomplished and mature we are—to the church, via its clergy (among other avenues) for healing and growth. Every parishioner is vulnerable and should be able to find a completely safe environment in which to heal.[29] Every pastor-parishioner romantic relationship is, on these grounds, potentially incestuous on a deep, unconscious level.

4. There is a desire on the part of clergy in many denominations to be more egalitarian in their relationships with parishioners. As a feminist and a respecter of group process, I agree that the foremost duty of clergy should always be to empower and equip the laity for leadership and ministry. However, empowering the laity for shared leadership does not mean divesting the clergy of their own distinctive role and power. The numinous role of the minister—particularly in his or her sacramental role—should preclude dating any parishioner. One cannot publicly and ritually mediate Christ, mediate the divine, for someone, for example, in the public celebration of the Eucharist, and be his or her lover at the same time. (For this reason I have also advocated that clergy spouses find their own separate pastoral support and even congregation, at least for part of the time.)

5. The prognosis for such relationships is poor. Those relationships that do not dissolve tend to perpetuate a power-over dynamic, and the parishioner remains vulnerable to exploitation within the relationship.[30]

6. Finally, there are serious negative consequences for the community of faith.[31] What does it mean to single out one parishioner for special love and intimacy? What does it say to others not chosen? What factions begin to be set up, pro and con, or aligning with one partner or the other? And what if the relationship breaks down? It is rare for the pastor to be the one to leave the parish if one party must leave. The potential for divisiveness, for people leaving hurt and angry, and for loss of trust and loss of community for the woman is tremendous. It cannot but harm the minister's own ministry in that place, and possibly for generations after him (or her).

For all these reasons, while we may be tempted to create loopholes in our ethics policies from a desire to be pastoral to everybody, including the clergy, we need a strong, unqualified standard—because especially from the perspective of victims, the potential for harm is otherwise too great.

Are Certain Women Predisposed to Becoming Victims?

There is no one type of woman predisposed to victimization by clergy. As in working with battered women, we know from experience that, contrary to prevailing myths and stereotypes, because of the way all of us, women and men, are socialized, any woman can be abused. There are, however, some generally learned susceptibilities that incline women to overlook, forgive, and tolerate a pastor's sexual exploitation:

1. socialization to be polite, nonconfrontational, accepting of men's behavior;

2. training and desire to heal men's wounds—offending clergy often present themselves to women as needing their special love and healing;

3. submissiveness as a Christian value, especially ingrained in church women;

4. identity defined for women by society as primarily sexual in function.

Particular life situations can add to a woman's vulnerability, and many clergy perpetrators have an uncanny knack—some women call it almost telepathic in intensity—for zeroing in on women with these vulnerabilities (partly because the intimate details are being shared with them in counseling):

1. divorce, marital conflict, or abuse;

2. a husband who shows indifference or is frequently absent—the pastor's interest in her as a person can be felt as needed validation and affirmation;

3. a time of career confusion—his encouragement is important to her;

4. decade transitions and aging (especially at midlife or older)—a powerful man who validates her attractiveness is affirmation for which she may hunger;

5. a new, young, or problem child—he makes her feel like a person in her own right again, not just an overburdened mother;

6. particular dedication to the church—this includes lay ministers, church committee members, employees, and seminary interns. Saying "no" or confronting him may carry risks of embarrassment or loss of community, livelihood, or ordination;

7. a personal history of family boundary violations—sexual, physical, or psychological—which makes it harder for her to have clarity about what is inappropriate on his part;

8. particular power differentials such as a large age difference, or if he has particular prominence in the community or denomination.

In short, virtually any life transition that brings a woman in to talk with her pastor can be exploited by a pastor to satisfying his own power needs at her expense.

Profile of Clergy Abusers

A number of explanations have been put forth for clergy crossing sexual boundaries with parishioners. Two typologies have become increasingly well known. Marie Fortune has described sexual abusers on a continuum between two types: "the wanderer," who "wanders across" boundaries, and the "predator," who seeks out victims deliberately and is lacking in conscience.[32] A sixfold typology based on extensive work in the field of clinical assessment and rehabilitation of offenders (including therapists and other professionals as well as clergy) has been developed by Gary Schoener: uninformed/naive, healthy or mildly neurotic, severely neurotic and/or socially isolated, impulsive character disorders, sociopathic or narcissistic character disorder.[33]

Such typologies have both advantages and disadvantages. They are useful because they give descriptive examples of clergy offenders that resonate well with the experience of victims and congregations. They bring more nuance and complexity into the work of understanding clergy who cross sexual boundaries. The disadvantage of typologies is that they can sometimes be misused by offenders to minimize, protect, and redefine their behavior in the most favorable light, by convincing others in authority that they fall on the "less serious" end of the typological spectrum.[34] The tendency to minimize often joins with the tendency of church leaders to see things in the most immediately forgiving and optimistic way available. Born out of an authentic desire to care for offenders, the culture of the church still predominantly wants to view the majority of offenders as "wanderers," or "naive," or "mildly neurotic." At least half of offenders, however, fall on the side of the spectrum of more serious woundedness, resulting professional impairment, and poor prognosis for rehabilitation.[35] The church's culture of optimism too often leads church officials to view many offenders incorrectly as belonging to "wanderer" or "neurotic" categories, where they are given inappro-priate latitude for supposed rehabilitation and rapid reinstatement. The pastor's remorse and contrition, assurances that he is in personal therapy, or a proposal for supervision and limitation of duties are frequently then seen as sufficient for reinstatement. While this demonstrates compassion for offenders, it all too often results in a trivialization of victims' complaints and the generation of more victims in years to come.

It may also be useful to understand clergy professional misconduct in terms of contributing factors, the more of which are present, the greater the likeli-hood that abuse has occurred or will occur in the future.[36] The advantage of this approach could be that it values the complexity and individuality of cases. The danger is that these factors might be used as excuses. Neither a typological model nor a model of multiple factors is intended to excuse behavior or to remove responsibility from the minister who crosses a professional boundary. Only with this caution in mind, a model of contributing factors might include: (1) educa-tional gaps, (2) situational stresses, (3) characterological factors resulting from psychological woundedness in many clergy.

Education

Until recently, the training of seminarians in professional ethics has been woe-fully lacking in most ministers' educations. Only in the last decade or so has the issue of professional boundaries been included in clergy training in most institu-tions, or in books for clergy.[37] Earlier mentions of sexual ethics tended to exclu-sively on sexual morality, not power and responsibility, and schools with more conservative theological frameworks re: traditional roles of men and women still tend to follow this model. In some cases, training has emphasized overcoming temptation and learning to resist feminine wiles.[38]

Lack of training has been, in some cases, compounded by confusion, beginning especially in the latter part of the 20th century, concerning sexual norms. Many clergy practicing today either received their initial training or passed through continuing education experiences during the late 1960s and early 1970s, when the helping professions in general were in a state of flux and experimentation. The clergy profession was giving increasing attention to the field of psychotherapy just at a time when the more abstinent methodology of psychoanalysis was being challenged on both professional and more popular fronts. The development of encounter groups, transactional analysis and group marathons, sex therapy, as well as vehement debates among psychotherapists about the possibility of touching clients (and more)[39] filtered into popular literature and had a formative influence on many clergy. Especially in liberal mainline denominations, such discussions gave tacit permission, and even supplied a rationale, for loosening traditional standards of sexual morality in the practice of ministry. Such discussions focused on the freeing effects of shedding repressive sexual conventions. Issues of the clergy's power as a professional and fiduciary responsibility were overlooked in the desire to seem modern and nonjudgmental.

Situational Factors

One situational factor, and the one most often cited as the cause of clergy sexual misconduct, is clergy stress. In particular, marital discord, workaholism, emotional enmeshment with the congregation, social isolation, loneliness, and lack of significant relationships, or loss of a parent or child, are cited as pushing vulnerable clergy over the edge into misconduct. The decline of public esteem of the clergy role has also been cited.[40] Burnout and overcommitment to work are frequently mentioned in connection with clergy dysfunction,[41] although some have questioned whether clergy stress has actually been overrated.[42]

Other external factors may also serve as disinhibitors for misconduct. The absence of supervision and accountability within the church setting, and the minister's unique access to vulnerable parishioners, including visits to their homes and bedsides, are further situational factors.

Alcohol or other addictions are sometimes cited in cases of misconduct. As in cases of rape or domestic violence, it is important to recognize that drinking, drug use, or even "sex and love addiction"[43] is not the cause of the abuse, although it is often used as the excuse. The common myth, often held by the wife and by the parish and the denomination, is: "Once he admits and deals with his alcohol problem, the sexual misconduct will stop." This can lead to unproductive treatment plans for the abuser, because the power dynamic of the abuse is deep-seated and independent of any substance abuse. It is more accurate to see alcohol as a *disinhibitor*—the clergyperson must already want to cross the boundary and feel on some level an entitlement to do so.

There is another situational factor as well, which is less often cited. An institutional culture of subordination and devaluation of women's experience, combined with a tolerance for sexual harassment and patriarchal sexual prerogative, also creates a powerful, if largely unspoken, situational factor. The relative social powerlessness of women to define their own boundaries and protest boundary invasions creates a climate where sexual abuse can thrive unspoken and unseen.[44] To the extent that the institution fails to convey or enforce a message that sexual abuse will have consequences, offenders will read an opposite message of tacit permission.

Wounded Clergy

Educational and situational factors alone do not explain clergy misconduct. While nearly all clergy are affected by at least some of these external factors, still approximately 80 to 90 percent of clergy do not cross sexual boundaries with parishioners. Internal factors, then, must also be considered.

The factor with the most predictive power for clergy sexual abuse is the woundedness of clergy. A number of mental health problems have been cited in cases of clergy abuse, from chronic depression and dependency, compulsive/ addictive personality, narcissism, "borderline" personality, to sociopathy and, in rare instances, psychosis. Some studies even suggest that the clergy profession may attract individuals at risk.[45]

And yet, even with this range of problems, not all neurotic or even disturbed clergy cross sexual boundaries, although they are supposedly at greater risk. For this reason, I also see a strong thread of narcissistic problems running through the entire range of clergy offenders.[46] Narcissism has its origin in the first years of life, and is therefore difficult to heal.[47] It impairs a minister's professional judgment in a way that puts him particularly at risk for crossing boundaries, because it damages his capacity for empathy and causes him to seek gratification of his own needs first, regardless of the cost to others. Even a "wanderer" or "neurotic" pastor may show narcissistic wounding through manipulative behavior, externalization of blame, and a tendency to use others especially in times of stress to meet personal needs.

Narcissism begins with early childhood wounding—sometimes quite subtle—in which the normal grandiosity of the very small child is crushed, leaving a great hole to be filled.[48] A mass of unconscious defendedness, like scar tissue, conceals this early wound, sometimes resulting in behavior that in turn victimizes others. Wants are seen through a distorted lens as needs. The narcissistically wounded professional tends to conceal his insecurities and cravings for attention under a behavioral style of entitlement and specialness—a style often condoned and even reinforced by the clergy role. At the mild end of the narcissism spectrum, a particular priest may become impatient because he does not feel he should have to stand in line at the bank, or make his own bed at a retreat center. At the extreme end is sociopathic behavior—an inability to feel empathy resulting in an absence of conscience. Because manipulation and the projection of a star image are common to narcissistically wounded people, empathy and conscience are often convincingly feigned. But deep in the person's soul is over-whelming despair, emptiness, and fear. For this reason, such individuals often have great difficulty establishing appropriate intimate relationships and friend-ships with male peers—often resulting in a "Lone Ranger" style of ministry.[49] Other people are used compulsively and heedlessly in a desperate attempt to keep the demons of worthlessness at bay.

The narcissistic clergy's personal craving for recognition combines explosively with the power of the clergy role and a social climate of masculine privilege. This helps to explain why clergy sexual abuse is, at its foundation, an abuse of power and not sex.

Why Don't Women Stop It or Report It?

A woman will often neither stop nor report clergy sexual abuse, for several rea-sons. First, she probably feels responsible. But as Marie Fortune has written, even if a woman initiated the sexual contact herself out of her own need or vul-nerability, it is the pastor's responsibility, just like a therapist's, to maintain the appropriate boundary. It was not her fault. And if she didn't, society still blames women for attracting men—the reason rape survivors usually feel that they are the ones on trial. This is further compounded by myths and stereotypes portray-ing all male pastors as innocent "sitting ducks" for the seductive wiles of female parishioners. The woman parishioner carries society's brand as the instigator of all sexual entanglements, still a prevalent theme in today's pastoral professional literature.[50] This is reinforced by a long woman-blaming tradition of romantic fiction portraying the virile but naive young pastor being preyed upon by sex-starved divorcees and overbearing wives.[51]

Victim-blaming, however, can also take the more sophisticated guise of clini-cal diagnoses of women, ranging from masochism and self-defeating personality disorder to "codependency," borderline personality, and woman-blaming-once-removed by blaming the perpetrator's mother for poor bonding and causing his narcissistic wounds! All such strategies serve to divert attention from the appro-priate focus: holding the abuser accountable for the abuse.

Second, a woman may fail to stop or report abuse because initially she feels validated by it on some level. It's flattering; it makes her feel special. At vulner-able times especially, this is compelling. Third, over time, her self-esteem is seriously battered down by this relationship, especially when, as often happens, his initial encouragement and validation give way to discounting and criticism. Fourth, once the sexual relationship is begun, the perpetrator will commonly engage in deliberately confusing behavior, or "crazy-making." Women have consistently reported extreme highs and lows in the relationship and an on-again, off-again quality. Promises of marriage are proffered and then withdrawn. Fifth, she is often sworn, with a religious intensity, to secrecy. "The parish would never understand our kind of love." "Only God understands." Sometimes, in the worst cases, this opens the door for multiple relationships with several parishioners at once.

The woman doesn't want to hurt his career. She loves him and believes he needs her. The good times make the bad times worth it—the good times are the "real him." She may be unwilling to hurt his wife and family or the church's reputation. Both his wife and the congregation would be quick to blame her as the source of their pain for bringing the truth to light, rather than placing the blame on the one who caused the abuse in the first place.

Finally, a woman may fail to stop or report abuse out of fear. Once a certain determination to think about leaving has taken hold in her, it is often fear that keeps her stuck: fear (often realistic) that no one will believe her side when it's her word against his; fear (often realistic) that she will be the one held responsible; fear (often realistic) of losing her attachment to that church, as well as sometimes the community in which she lives, her personal reputation, and, if she is employed there, her own professional reputation; and even fear of his retaliation—sometimes within the sphere of personal and church life, but also sometimes toward the end there are actual instances of physical violence, rape, or threats of violence, and women have reason to fear them. Perhaps most chilling and most unique to clergy abuse is the fear of violation or retaliation on the spiritual level. This became increasingly clear to me in work with survivors' groups. It is difficult for a nonsurvivor to comprehend the sheer terror that accompanies this form of abuse. But often because of the image of charismatic spiritual power that these clergymen have asserted and fostered, there can be a terror akin actually to being cursed or damned. Sometimes this kind of threat is almost made explicitly by the abuser, treading dangerously close to the realm of ritualistic abuse. Its power is clearly demonic in nature and intensity—victims fear that their very souls will be stolen.

The Clergy Nightmare: False Allegations

This is a common fear, and some conscientious clergy may feel overly constrained in their pastoral relationships by their denomination's sexual ethics policies, for fear of false allegations or of having genuine warmth and concern misconstrued as a sexual advance. However, most denominational executives and professional counselors working with cases of abuse will state that, in their experience, victims are so frightened and ashamed that they are much more likely to minimize and deny their experience than to inflate it or make false accusations. Cases of disturbed individuals making false charges are rare.[52] The fear among clergy is often fueled by false "information": for example, the myth of the predatory female who, especially if scorned, will turn and cry rape (sometimes invoking the biblical story of Potiphar's wife in Genesis 39:7-20[53]); the sensationalism surrounding rare cases of false accusation; and especially the rampant denial about real cases—including perpetrator-colleagues' convincing retellings of what occurred—which are then dismissed as false allegations by entire communities.

There is no doubt that false allegations can be devastating both to clergy and to congregations. If a minister is concerned about this issue with a specific parishioner, it is well to err on the side of caution to maintain extra vigilance about boundaries—emotional, physical, and psychological[54]—and to make careful use of good supervision/consultation. It is helpful to clergy worried about this to keep two things in mind: first, that any woman who actually approaches her pastor sexually is often sending a signal for help and needs appropriate and compassionate support and boundaries[55]; second, that, given the severe scrutiny to which even legitimate complaints are subjected, false allegations are extremely unlikely to stand.[56] Documenting confusing interactions, telling a supervisor, and seeking peer and/or professional consultation are all healthy safeguards in situations where a pastor feels uncomfortable about a parishioner's behavior.

Helping the Survivor

As with other forms of abuse described in previous chapters, the most important messages are: "I believe you," "I am so sorry—in the name of the church that I love and serve—that this happened to you," and "No matter what sense of responsibility you feel, it is always the clergyperson's responsibility as a professional to maintain the boundaries: it is not your fault." Validate her feelings, which may include rage, fear, grief, guilt, and shame. Be alert to threats from the abuser—even threats of physical violence have been known to occur once the survivor decides to make a report. Help her think through an action plan should retaliation begin to emerge. Do not offer forgiveness unless she asks you for it, and even then let her know that sexual abuse is not her fault. Assist her in finding an advocate within the denominational system who can accompany her through the process if she chooses to report. Reporting is not a light matter. Perhaps the most important conviction a survivor needs to carry with her into any formal proceeding is that she is deciding to report for the sake of her own integrity, and not because she needs or expects the institution to respond perfectly (it won't), or the abusing clergyperson to "see the light," repent, and change (rare).[57] As in pastoral care with victims of other forms of violence, it is critical to respect her self-determination in this regard. The victim's safety is the first priority.[58]

Prevention and Intervention with Clergy

Prevention

The discussion above of factors contributing to clergy misconduct has implications for prevention and intervention. Most prevention programs currently being implemented tend to focus on improving education and remedying situational problems. This is important work. Some prevention education focuses mainly on avoiding legal liability or on learning a set of safety rules (such as never closing the door while providing pastoral care—of course, for the safety and confidentiality of the parishioner, one must be able to provide privacy). Knowing safeguards is important.[59] However, genuine predators are adept at circumventing rules and restrictions. The most effective education emphasizes not solely *what* clergy can do, but *how* they are to think about themselves, their strengths and weaknesses, their role as clergy, and issues of gender, power, and authority.

One diocesan committee framed preventive measures in the helpful terms of "habits of mind": cultivating a habit of self-questioning, recognition of danger signals, and a framework of containment, peer supervision, and checks and balances for accountability.[60] Clergy need to acknowledge and accept rather than suppress personal feelings, including a calm awareness that sexual feelings will sometimes develop,[61] but, importantly, they must then be able to distinguish between feelings and behavior and take responsibility for acting appropriately.[62] Clergy should be prepared for this. William Hulme writes:

> Charles Rassieur in his book, *The Problem Clergymen Don't Talk About* (1976), quotes a pastor in regard to a woman counselee, "Hey, she turns me on! I wonder what's going to happen now?" (71). Anybody who has to wonder

about this is ill prepared for any vocation in which responsibility is expected. This is a question that needs to be faced and resolved when one accepts the call to be ordained. It is a question of identity. If you know who you are, you will not wonder what will happen when you become turned on by another with whom you are involved in a ministerial function. You will know.[63]

Clergy also need to know what forms of pastoral counseling are beyond their training and professional experience, and have clarity about when to refer parishioners for psychotherapy.[64]

Yet even this good training is not sufficient. If woundedness of clergy is the most predictive factor for abuse, then programs for clergy wellness, beginning at the seminary level, are crucial. Further, if a majority of offenders are troubled by characterological problems stemming from narcissistic wounding, even clergy wellness programs will not be able to prevent abuse in many instances. This reality raises the need for much greater vigilance at the threshold of ministry, including more rigorous testing and screening of candidates for ministry. Both seminaries and denominational commissions on ministry need to empower themselves to recognize the early warning signs and to counsel at-risk candidates away from the helping professions, toward more appropriate work. Ordination is a privilege, not a right. It is not "unpastoral" to redirect a candidate for ministry toward a different vocation. In fact, it is more pastoral *to* do so, both for the sake of the aspirant, and the safety of his potential future parishioners.

Intervention

1. *At the outset, if there is a presenting problem of alcohol, family disruption, or financial impropriety, or a parish dynamic of secrecy and closed or chaotic process, it is important to be alert to possible sexual abuse.* A typical indicator of abuse in a parish is multilayered confidentiality, a lot of gossip, and just a few people in an inner circle "in the know." A healthy parish dynamic, in contrast, would be one where decision-making processes are transparent, there are no intentional secrets (although confidentiality, as in pastoral and personnel matters, is observed respectfully and according to stated policies), and business is conducted openly.

2. *Where there is one kind of boundary violation, expect to find others.* For example, sexual abuse of parishioners often goes hand in hand with unethical personnel practices (such as nepotism and gender discrimination in general), lying, and financial abuses.

3. *Once sexual abuse has been identified, expect minimization and denial, expect to be diverted onto issues of alcohol abuse or extreme stress, and don't lose sight of the power pattern that is really operative and needs to remain the focus of treatment.* To

join in minimizing the offending clergyperson's responsibility is inadvertently to reinforce his behavior.

Treatment programs that explain the underlying problem of clergy offenders solely as "sexual addiction" or "sex and love addiction"[65] are not appropriate. The term "sexual addiction" misleadingly frames the clergyperson's misconduct in terms of a physiological disease, like alcoholism, which may further distance him from taking responsibility for his behavior. Sexual misconduct and exploitation of power will not stop until it is dealt with directly as such. A purely addiction-model treatment will not address a male power addiction, because the dependency model does not delve deeply enough into confronting the root societal forces that keep male power over women in place and name it normal.

4. *Give an unequivocal message that all sexual or romantic relating with parishioners is wrong.* Educate him about why it is wrong and about the socialization that has harmfully made it seem acceptable. Society conditions and socializes young men to see women as sexual prey, seductresses who will say "no" and mean "yes." Help him to see how this has harmed his ability to relate to women and thus harmed his ministry—and his life.

5. *Avoid collusion.*[66] What does a clergyperson do upon finding out that one of his or her colleagues is abusing a parishioner or parishioners? Depending on the denomination's polity, usually the best route is to go to one's bishop or equivalent judicatory officer for pastoral advice, and let him or her handle the matter. Confronting the abusing clergyperson first is not necessarily the best choice of action, unless one feels quite safe doing so. Beyond one's own personal safety, it is absolutely necessary to strictly respect the safety of the victim. It is important to share the policies and procedures of the denomination with her, if such policies exist, and let her know how to access the complaint procedures, if any. If she has reported the abuse to you and has asked you to keep it in confidence, it is possible to ask her permission to share it with the bishop or other executive or designated person. If she says no, keep supporting her process, but respect her wishes and follow her own instincts about what is safest for her—knowing that she may fear reprisals. If she has not reported, but you have found out another way, you might take the information to bishop judicatory officer for advice, without revealing the victim's identity. However, absent a formal complaint from a victim, little or nothing can be done unless there is compelling third-party evidence. And even without naming the victim, revealing details may expose her to retaliation by the offender. In all cases, the victim's safety must come first. The best safeguard against collusion is remembering to whom we owe our first loyalty—to the victims, both present and future.

6. *Arrange for disclosure of the abuse to the congregation*, without naming victims. A public forum in which the whole congregation can air their feelings and questions, without debate and in an atmosphere carefully structured to provide safety for all participants, further reinforces a "zero tolerance" stance toward clergy misconduct. Disclosure reverses the patterns of secrecy and obfuscation that misconduct engenders. Congregations where no disclosure occurs have no opportunity to process the trauma to the congregational system, and a poisonous brew of rumors and unspoken fears and memories often ensues, with the potential to stifle growth, inhibit communication, and contaminate subsequent pastoral relations for generations. Such disclosure should be done by an experienced and trained member of a judicatory staff—or preferably a multidisciplinary team that also includes mental health professionals[67]—who can balance the limits of confidentiality with appropriate transparency, are knowledgeable about congregational dynamics, and have some experience with systems-level interventions. Best practices for disclosure follow a trauma debriefing model where the range of feelings that can exist among members of the community can be shared without fear of judgment and thus "normalized" as valid crisis responses.[68] Disclosures will inevitably displease some people at all levels of the church—including at times some church insurers and attorneys![64]—but in the long run, the failure to help the congregation to work through their pain, anger, and betrayal will have more far-reaching consequences.

The Development of Policy: An Institutional Mandate

Churches need ethical codes that accurately name and recognize the prevalence of the problem. Most mainline Protestant churches now have policies and procedures, and many other denominations are currently developing them, as churches are increasingly facing the reality of clergy sexual abuse—and are being called to legal, financial, and, most of all, moral responsibility for professional clergy who minister in the name of Christ. Many models are now available.[69] but this is still a pioneering time. Many policies established in the 1990s continue to lack clarity, even about what types of behaviors constitute misconduct, or what the process will be once a complaint is brought.[70] Many new policies and procedures are still being tested and refined, even as more women are being given the institutional message that it may be safe to come forward with their stories.

At minimum, denominational policies should include:[71]

(1) Recognition of the prevalence of the problem and the need for a policy, including theological rationale;

(2) A clear standard of behaviors in each judicatory body of each denomination with a clear disciplinary process that holds the pastor responsible for *all* sexual boundary violations.[72] (In most states, it will be essential that denominations take the initiative to adopt such policies, since attempts to legislate pastoral professional ethics, similar to laws regulating professional behavior of therapists and medical practitioners, have been blocked by church lobbies on the grounds of separation of church and state.) Because blurring of boundaries and role confusion have been shown to contribute to clergy misconduct, the respective roles and expectations for both training and conduct of ordained and lay leaders should be clearly defined[73];

(3) Mandatory training of clergy and lay leaders in positions of authority, including requirements for regular refresher training (e.g., every five years).[74]

(4) An established program for investigation, processing, and healing for congregations in which abuse has occurred,[75] and specialized training for interim clergy and "after pastors" whose job it will be to help a congregation heal from betrayal;

(5) Justice rather than only sympathy for victims—including clear policies and procedures for the support of victims and mechanisms for restitution. Having victim advocates or ombudspersons in place is often the best mechanism for offering appropriate, confidential support;

(6) Clear consequences, which include accurate public naming of the problem, some form of censure or suspension with the goal of preventing harm to others, required evaluation during and at the conclusion of treatment, and appropriate restitution to victims.[76] As Barbara Blodgett has written, "one way to minimize the risk of harm is to be ready for it. . . . Adopting a response plan for misconduct also communicates a clear message that the community will not tolerate it."[77]

(7) Consequences should include reeducation/resocialization, rather than just sympathy, much less collusion, for the perpetrator. State-of-the-art assessment by a specialist with expertise in professional misconduct and treatment for those deemed treatable should be assigned by the denomination. The denomination should have appropriate referrals established prior to any complaint. In conjunction with this treatment, the local church and denominational office has an *ongoing responsibility* for monitoring that treatment process rather than simply referring and "being done with it," and, as Marie Fortune has advocated, for establishing clear and well-publicized consequences;

(8) Publication of policies and procedures, with clear steps for reporting and recourse for all parties, made available and visible on web sites, in

denominational new media, and in all congregations. As Christie Neuger has argued, congregations *as well as* individual church leaders need information about appropriate boundaries, and personnel committees in particular should be trained to recognize warning signs of poor boundaries, such as "excessive self-disclosure, impulsive touch, meeting with people in times or in places outside the norm, engaging in secrecy, engaging in self-serving behaviors, and so forth."[78] Congregational leaders can also become better educated about the ways in which the congregational system can either collude with or actively work to prevent clergy sexual abuse.[79]

(9) A standard procedure for disclosure to congregations, as described above.

(10) Finally, all policies and procedures should be backed up by a demonstrated commitment to practices of equality throughout the denomination and its member congregations. To quote Neuger again,

> Judicatories need to re-think the explicit and implicit models of ministry they see as normative. Questions for exploring these normative models of ministry might include: How do our faith groups understand religious leadership? What messages do we send about isolation, work pressures, and support systems? How do we communicate and demonstrate appropriately transparent power relationships, including those that are culturally-based? Judicatories need to make their values apparent by actively supporting healthy and ethical behaviors in clergy and by making the consequences for unethical behaviors clear and consistent.[80]

In conclusion, nothing less than a total paradigm shift is needed, from treating the problem as one only of sexual morality, emotional instability, or addiction, to addressing the power dynamics of these often hidden abuses. Only as this begins to happen throughout all denominations, and the church removes its rose-colored lenses of denial and collusion, can the church community be a place of authentic power, healing, and proclamation for both women and men.

Part Two
The Experience of Abuse

9

When Faith Is Twisted

ANNETTE ANDERSON*

I didn't see it coming. I never imagined myself vulnerable to sexual temptation, much less to an extra-marital relationship. When I fell into one with my pastor, the effect on my life was devastating.

My church had problems which created a ripe environment for spiritual abuse. Its emphasis on *perfect* behavior and a *prophetic* connection to God laid a dangerous foundation. Words such as *authority*, *obey*, *submit*, and *power* were loaded with implications which served our leaders' objective to take us in any direction they wanted to go.

Insulated from most outside influence, independent thoughts and opinions were not welcome in our church community. Anyone who voiced concern for the direction we were heading was labeled an agent of Satan. Our defensive and spiritually superior culture became an increasingly toxic environment.

The youngest of our three pastors was a breath of fresh air in the mix. Enthusiastic and visionary, he seemed especially eager to sacrifice everything for God and encouraged others to do the same. Fueled by an experience where God had spared his life as an infant, his charisma and passion were inspiring to those of us he visited on a near daily basis.

I'm not sure when he began to turn his attention toward me in an inappropriate way. He was always a bit over the top, but at the time, I didn't think twice about it. Whether blinded by gratitude for the counseling sessions which miraculously saved my marriage, or his constant offers to babysit my kids, one thing's for sure—the words *predator, grooming,* and *cult* were not part of my vocabulary—otherwise I'd have run the other way.

The sudden death of my pastor's young wife devastated our church community. Yet he seemed to prophetically foresee the tragedy coming. *The fire had been so hot,* he told me through tears; *there was nothing left of her.* He was so strong—another sign of his profound connection with God. But he'd need my help to get through his grief. God *told him* this would be allowed and for me to withhold my comfort would be *selfishness* on my part, which would ultimately displease God.

---

* A pseudonym.

God is doing something new here. I don't know why this is allowed, but I know it is God. God's showing his love through me; this must be why she had to die…

My pastor's words were beyond persuasive—they were directive. His life-long special connection to God assured me that he knew better than I. The fact that morality was relative to a higher way of spiritual thinking was something I'd never before considered, yet many things preached from our pulpit seemed to confirm that God's methods were subject to change.

Would I help God's new work, or hinder it? Comfort a man in his darkest hour, or participate in his persecution? Was I in, or would I be outside of God's new move? The choice was mine, or so I thought, and I wouldn't say *no* to God.

He arranged our rendezvous in a hotel room far away from our church community. This confused me. I wasn't sure why we'd sneak around if this was part of *what God was doing*. Meeting for sex became a regular occurrence between my pastor and me.

Attention from other women also became needed by him, due to hostile accusations coming his way. The exact nature of these accusations was vague to me as most of my information came from him. According to my pastor—he was suffering from acute spiritual persecution in addition to his grief-stricken state of widowhood. He needed, and was entitled to, all the *comfort* he could get.

My pastor's spiritualization of sex had a devastating impact on my life. I couldn't reconcile what was happening to me. Despite all attempts to rationalize it, sin was still sin, and its destructive force worked into every crevice of my soul, mind, and spirit. I eventually became housebound with depression and, to the neglect of my husband and three small children, rarely got out of bed.

Cigarettes replaced food, and alcohol released my mind from its tortured state of confusion and regret. Fearing my deteriorated state a threat to his own survival, my pastor paired me with a pseudo-friend—another woman with whom he'd also been having a sexual relationship—a fact I did not realize at the time. Her presence was comforting. Together, we seemed barely able to survive.

Between the sudden death of the pastor's young wife, accusations of his involvement with several women, and some power maneuvering between the three pastors of our troubled church, life was rapidly falling apart on all counts.

For reasons only God knows, I began to read my Bible again. What I found on its pages in no way matched the road my life had taken. Through his Word the Lord began to realign my moral compass, showing me his boundaries for not only sex, but for the proper use of power and the right treatment of others. My fog cleared as I realized the magnitude of abuses within my church.

I recognized my need to get away from the twisted influence of my pastor and sought help from a professional counselor—an act which saved my life. Eventually I mustered the courage to move away and end all contact with him.

The next several years took twists and turns I'd never imagined. My pastor was arrested, tried, and convicted for the murder of his wife. Her death was the result of an alliance between him and the woman with whom he'd paired me. Chilling details of the murder and sexual abuses still challenge my perceptions of Christianity.

Since this trauma, I've found a relationship with the true Jesus of the Bible. I've learned that those who use church to gain power and access to unsuspecting and vulnerable people will ultimately answer to God for it.

Above all, I'm grateful that the Lord saved me and restored my family. May his good work endure forever.

10

A Simple Procedure

Desiree' Kameka

I share my story because I believe the leaders of the church should hear one real outcome of the church's harsh judgment, and its lack of true compassion for those who have struggled with the decision of abortion.

It is amazing that somewhere in between classes and nightclubs, I became Christian. I wanted all of my friends to experience this new sense of peace and belonging, not to "save them from hell," but because I experienced a psycho-spiritual shift that was unlike any other life giving experience I had felt in the past. During that time, the Holy Spirit was transforming my identity, but I was listening to humans who were telling me how to be a "good Christian" instead of investigating Jesus myself.

I decided to stop taking my birth control pills since as a "good Christian" I would not be having sex with anyone anymore. Well, I ended up meeting a pastor's son and getting pregnant. I was terrified. How could I tell my new Christian friends that I was having sex, let alone pregnant! They would know I was a failure and would never accept me. My boyfriend told his father, the pastor, as we knew he would support our decision to have the child. Surprisingly, we were told that having a child at our age and out of wedlock would be unwise and that he could not help us because he had the church and the rest of his family to care for.

Feeling as if I had no support and or guidance, I decided I had no choice. I must have an abortion. Alone and scared I drove up to the clinic, praying that the Pro-Life/anti-abortion protestors would not be standing on the corner. I didn't need my shame to be rubbed in my face. I needed someone to hold my hand, give me other options and support my decision to have the baby. A knot balled up in my throat as I checked-in with the receptionist. She handed me forms and told me, "Everything will be ok, it's a simple procedure." Filling out the release papers, tears welled up in my eyes. I was raised in a home that supported the local Hope Pregnancy Center. I knew getting an abortion was wrong, but I convinced myself that things were more complicated now and that my parents would never understand or forgive me for letting them down.

The smell of surgical gloves and blaring blue flower-print walls made me nauseous. Trying to avoid eye contact, several other women shared the small waiting room and would soon share the same experience. Looking toward the nurse, I desperately wanted her to say something that would motivate me to walk out, but she nonchalantly put on a movie that explained the procedure and post-operative healing instructions.

After the video, which I half watched, she walked us down a long beige hallway, placing us in separate rooms. I wondered if the woman in front of me was feeling the same numbness I was. Sitting down naked on the cold metal operating table, I felt completely exposed and empty. I didn't even realize I was crying until the doctor walked in and told me not to worry assuring me that everything would be over soon.

He lied to me. I woke up dazed, sitting in a recliner next to the nurses' station, and then drove myself home. The procedure was over, but it was just the beginning of a long road to healing. No one told me that my body would continue to change, that my mind would replay that day over and over, that my faith in God and humanity would be shattered, that I would go into a lonely depression not being able to grieve with anyone for fear of rejection and judgment. Even now, seven years later, I can't help but look at a toddler and imagine that I should be raising my own. I will never forget my first child and continue to grieve my loss.

I wrote a healing poem one day after solitary prayer: "I got your letter . . ."

> Mommy do you know
> How much I love you so
> How I love to sit and watch you
> And all the lovely seed you sow?
> Mommy do you know
> You don't have to cry for me?
> I'm safe and sound in Jesus arms
> Wrapped in sweet serenity
> Mommy do you know
> How much I love you so
> In all your laughter and your tears
> I cheer you in all your victories
> I hold you in all your fears
> I know how much you love me
> By the things you say and do

I'm so glad that you're my mommy
I can't wait to be held by you!
Mommy I know you miss me
But the future is for eternity
You'll have all the time in the world
To get to know me . . .
Your little girl. . . . Your Trinity.

As a Christian, I knew what I was doing was wrong and I was heartbroken, but I felt as if I had no choice. If just one person came up to me and gave me a hug, held my trembling hand, and asked if I wanted to look at other options, I would have in a heartbeat. Have Christians forgotten the words of 1 John 3:18, "Dear children, let us not love with words or speech but with actions and in truth"? There is no evidence that Jesus ever stigmatized the sexually suspect. Instead, he went out of his way to extend grace, and was often rebuked for his kindness to them. Should not my pastor and Christian friends, as the Body of Christ, be the ones to whom I could turn, knowing that they would extend the accepting hand of Christ to me? Why should I still sit alone and silent when many other women have shared my same experience?

The church's refusal to deal with issues of sexuality openly and through the lens of love has resulted in both the spiritual and the physical death of many. Lord, have mercy on us.

11

He Led Us to Salvation

K. J. NADISHA*

I t was past midnight when I went to sleep on a mattress on the floor. I had packed away our furniture, since we were moving overseas. My husband had already left a day earlier with my other children, and I was due to follow with my daughter, who was sleeping in her room at the far side of the house. I was exhausted, and I fell asleep wearing one of my husband's t-shirts.

I awoke to discover my pastor on top of me. I was lying on my back. My shirt was still on but had been lifted.

He was naked. I had not heard him enter my home or enter my room or undress. As I was waking up, I was a little hazy and trying to remember where I was and what was happening. He was having sex with me. I was shocked. I could not react. He was breathing heavily. He said, "Sshhh."

It all happened so quickly. He fell heavily on me. His breath was hot and damp on my neck. It was so surreal. I couldn't speak. He said that I was so attractive and irresistible. I heard him saying about needing badly to connect with me for one last time before I left to go overseas.

Since the first time he had raped me, I had never consented to have sex with him. This time he had come into my house. His clothes were on the floor, near the door. He had a yellow shirt and trousers with a heavy belt, shoes and socks.

Once he got up, I lay there sobbing. He was telling me to clean myself up so my daughter would not be traumatized by seeing me like that. Somehow I got to the shower. My daughter walked into the bathroom hugging her white teddy bear. She said that the pastor was in the house and he was waiting to take us to the airport.

I was numb with shock, but I was able to check my daughter was okay. I tried hard to conceal my distress.

The pastor then drove us to the airport. He said that he wanted to take us to the airport, even if this made his wife jealous and angry. His wife was calling and sending him messages. He answered the calls. The pastor showed me one

---

* A pseudonym.

91

of the text messages that she sent to him. It said she cared for him too much for her own good.

At last, we were on the plane and escaping to safety. Once we landed, I phoned the pastor to confront him about the rape and that he had betrayed my trust in him.

He promised never to have sex with me again. He phoned again and again apologizing and justifying his actions. He said my husband had given him the keys to our house so he could take us to the airport. He admitted he had opened the door and when he saw me he could not resist. He quoted scriptures to try to justify what he did to me.

I still wanted to believe that he would not intentionally hurt me. I had not been exposed to Christian teachings until arriving in Australia to live with my husband and children. He taught that to follow Jesus Christ meant we must forgive each other every sin against us. He begged for forgiveness. He blamed me for causing his temptation.I blamed myself and tried to avoid being attractive. Nothing worked.

I was unable to name his sins as crime. He had led me to denounce the faith I was practicing since birth and embrace the eternal salvation of Jesus. He had baptized my daughter and renewed my husband's faith in Christ. He offred spiritual guidance and groomed me and my husband to be spiritually and emotionally dependent on him.

How could I refuse to forgive him when he cried and pleaded with me? He had taught us that unforgiveness would condemn me and my family to hell. He told me Satan was trying to break my family away from God.

Through support from advocates and counselors, I eventually saw through his lies and realized he was a criminal, taking advantage of vulnerable women in churches. He had been caught before but neither prosecuted by the police nor disciplined by the church. I began to grow strong, as I reported him to police and had him prosecuted.

I am finally free to understand that his crimes were his crimes and I had done nothing to provoke him.

My husband and children have supported me through the prosecution. Now I can speak for other silent victims of clergy sexual crimes, knowing that Jesus is beside me, making me strong against an insidious evil.

12

Unjust Systems

Amanda Gearing

The trial in Australia of a former senior Baptist pastor on twenty-one sex and violence charges last year marked a low-point in public confidence for the Baptist Union and, by implication, other churches in Australia rocked by the continuing procession of clerics of various denominations being jailed for sex crimes.

The pastor in this case was acquitted of all charges. However, his admissions of extramarital sex with a vulnerable parishioner sent shock waves through congregations and the clergy. The former pastor, who is married with children, led a Perth congregation for six years. His confessions in the court to engaging in an extramarital affair came as a deep shock to the faithful congregation who heard him preach about the sanctity of marriage.

The Baptist Churches of Western Australia has a ChurchSafe program designed to stamp out abuse in the church. ChurchSafe warns ministers to behave with integrity because their personal behaviour and relationships are a model to others and therefore have a significant impact on the church and the community. The program also sets out clear standards of conduct for ministers requiring them to display behaviours and attitudes that are above reproach when interacting with others and to be sensitive and respectful towards people with different family and cultural traditions.

For the faithful congregations, shock may turn to anger in this case, however, because the congregation "forgave" the pastor for a previous adulterous affair he confessed to having with a parishioner in Queensland. The Baptist Union might find it difficult to justify why they allowed a person known to have already violated ministerial standards, to be appointed as a church leader. Professional codes of behaviour in the medical profession, allied health and churches are designed to protect vulnerable patients, clients and parishioners.

In this case, the parishioner was far more vulnerable than an Australian woman would have been.

She was a recent immigrant to Australia from a devout Hindu tradition and with no understanding of Christian teachings. When she arrived at the church with her husband and two toddlers, she was heavily pregnant and had no extended family. The power structure of the relationship in this case was far more akin to clerical abuse of a child than an extramarital affair with an adult.

In clergy-child abuse, the abusive relationship is characterised by the grooming of all the protectors of the child, such as the parents and their colleagues, long before the offender begins any abuse of the target victim. Once the child's protectors develop trust in the clergy offender, the offender befriends the targeted child using gifts and attention.In addition, the cleric is in a position of spiritual authority, recognised by the victim's family and friends as being trustworthy, honest and faithful to Christian values. The child, once victimised, has no one to turn to, to report the evil they are experiencing.

In the Perth case, the same grooming procedure was carried out. The woman was introduced to scripture references on love and forgiveness which trapped her into silence in a maelstrom of shame, fear and confusion. That the case did reach a trial is due in large part to the woman's resolve to escape the imposed silence she had endured for several years. Once she escaped from the relationship in 2006, she graduated from university with a doctorate degree and threw herself into helping victims of child prostitution in developing countries. She has become a regular contributor to global forums and conferences, receiving several prestigious government awards and commendations at state, national and global level for her contributions to multicultural awareness.

Eventually she summoned the courage to report to police, made a statement running more than 250 pages, waited for a police investigation to be carried out and court processes to unfold.

After four years, the trial was finally underway and she was ready to give her evidence. What she did not expect from the trial of the offender, was to feel as though she was the one on trial, facing questioning about intimate details of the alleged sexual violence, and for her evidence to be subjected to the public glaze by being reported, and misreported, in the media. The pastor had had his name suppressed throughout the court proceedings. The suppression order was lifted at the beginning of the trial in the Perth District Court after *The West Australian* successfully argued that in the interests of open justice, his name should be released for publication.In an unusual move, the accused's legal counsel asked the court to allow the accused a day before his name was published because he had not yet told his aged father or his work colleagues of the serious charges against him. The court granted the extra time.

Despite the lifting of the suppression order, however, *The West Australian* still did not publish the name of the accused for fear of identifying the complainant in the case. Wanting extra legal protection, the newspaper asked the victim to sign a consent form to protect the newspaper in case she was identified by the details given in court reports. The consent form request coincided with a serious error in day one of the reporting of the case, when the reporter wrongly stated that the prosecution case was that the pastor had begged the woman not to have an abortion when he discovered she was pregnant. Whilst the reporter could be forgiven for assuming the pastor's stance on abortion, it was wrong. In fact the prosecution case was the exact opposite—that the pastor ordered the woman to have an abortion and threatened to kill himself unless she complied immediately. The woman, who had been deeply traumatised by unwillingly submitting to the abortion, was re-traumatised by having to write an extensive police statement outlining 21 sex and violence offences she alleged had been committed against her.

However, this paled to insignificance when compared with her horror at reading the false report published state-wide in the newspaper. The newspaper did not make a correction but tried to undo the damage by getting the story correct in their report of the case the following day.

She found the false reporting difficult to endure because there was no avenue for her to protect herself against the incorrect reporting. She gave her evidence in the court over nine days as she recounted the allegations and was cross-examined on two counts of aggravated burglary, one of assault occasioning bodily harm, eleven alleged rapes and seven indecent assaults. Several times during cross-examination she vomited when appalling propositions were put to her by the defence barrister. She almost gave up the case. Some mornings she felt unable to get out of bed, she trembled and cried at night recalling the day's brutal cross-examination. Yet she somehow managed to go back to the court day after day. She was determined to speak the truth as best she knew how—and she knew that as she spoke, she was a voice for the many victims of sex crimes who never have the opportunity to speak in court.

The reporter covering the trial was asked to cover other cases at the same time so he could not be in the court for the whole trial. The coverage did not include the weight of evidence from the accused and defense witnesses which demonstrated the deceptive nature of the accused's relationship with his wife, his church congregation, the complainant and her family. These deceptions were obvious to people in the courtroom. The reporting belittled and humiliated the complainant.

Some of the failure of the prosecution case was due to inadequate police investigation which arguably could have left reasonable doubt in the minds of the jury. The second investigating police officer admitted under cross-examination during the trial that he had failed to carry out vital investigations and had failed to gather critical evidence. *The West Australian* reported: A police detective admitted under cross-examination that he had never visited the woman's house or sought proof she had an abortion.Once the acquittal was delivered, the complainant felt, understandably, that the time she had spent in the witness box retelling and reliving her ordeal had come to naught. In addition, her unwillingness to sign the consent form meant the pastor was still not identified in the public arena.

Once the pastor was acquitted the newspaper decided not to name him, even though by then the complainant had regathered her strength and had signed the consent form.It appears the pastor has escaped unscathed. He now works as a real estate agent and his website claims that his "role of Senior Pastor at Baptist Churches around Australia has given him extra insight into human behaviour and the need for communication and trust." What is more surprising than the acquittal in this case is that the case proceeded to a court at all. Though the complainant is understandably disillusioned with the press and the acquittal, she is not crushed. She has already used her experiences to bring hope to women and children who are survivors of abuse, through arts and culture. Her advocacy on behalf of victims will be all the more powerful for her first-hand experience of the justice system. However, her estimation of Australia has been damaged and the family has moved overseas because they no longer feel safe in Australia.

The woman will undoubtedly speak of her experiences in global forums and work for change to protect other vulnerable people. Her husband, an Englishman with a doctoral degree, has supported his wife through the protracted prosecution and has seen her endure intolerable humiliation during the court case. He now understands how vulnerable his wife was when she attended a Christian church in a culture foreign to her Asian background seeking to assimilate herself and her children into the Australian culture. "My wife simply needed a place where she could pray and befriend Australians safely," he said. The husband and wife both relied on the congregation as their primary social network. The pastor became the husband's only trusted friend. "I was blinded by his position of spiritual authority and unable to protect my wife in spite of her numerous attempts to reach out to me," he said.

Having seen the suffering his wife endured and his own vulnerability, he is now supporting efforts to eliminate violence against women. "I don't want to see any woman suffer like my wife has suffered."

13

Giving Evidence

REX HOST

As a Christian, I firmly believe that there must be a way to stop the power abuse that leads to exploitation of vulnerable women by leaders in our churches. Yes, the issue may be complex for anyone who trust ministers and does not understand that the power entrusted to them can be easily abused. There are many who share my conviction but feel powerless.

But I know of one courageous women who is making a significant impact.

Last year, I witnessed this woman speaking out about her own experience of clergy abuse in an Australian court room. I felt her pain as I heard her reliving traumatic encounters of horrific and repeated violence and humiliation. I heard of her shame and the many attempts to stop the violence go in vain. I heard her account of the former pastor's repeated use of scriptures to demand her silence and forgiveness. I heard of her isolation and fear of being rejected by the church community and being blamed for ruining God's church. Her family, who were new to Australia, were very involved with the church community that had embraced them. The pastor had baptized her child and led them all to the salvation of Jesus. I watched helplessly as the judicial system allowed the defense to repeatedly violate her all over again within the so-called-security of the court system. I saw her endure horrible propositions used by the defense—so shocking that they caused her to break down numerous times in cross-examination and after several days on the stand was quite visibly and understandably weak. The church provided her no public support and did not seek to comfort her family. She was alone in giving evidence as she had been alone when her pastor abused her. During the court hearing, members of the church come forth to give witness in support of the pastor. This pastor and the church did untold spiritual damage. They were on the on the side of the one who had done horrible things to her. They were the representatives of God.

Yet this woman's credibility and integrity remained unwavering throughout the trial. Her advocacy for victims was now all the more powerful for her first-hand experience of embedded injustice within the church and the justice system.

Instead of giving up on churches, she gave a voice to all those who are voiceless and urging churches to address this issue. She has opened the eyes of many Christians and non-Christians who can refuse to succumb to the threats and pressures to remain silent on the violence against vulnerable women and children that continues to be perpetrated in the church of Jesus.

I found myself uncontrollably shedding tears when I called to thank her. I pledged to oppose violence against women and to prevent the cover-up of clergy abuse of women in churches.

My love for the church is not destroyed by the continuing abuse by ministers who use God's name to sanction their own evil deeds in churches. On the contrary, they now drive me harder to ensure that churches can be safe havens for the lost and downtrodden.

14

The Journey beyond Betrayal

ANN KENNEDY

I am a clergy abuse survivor. In my early twenties I joined a charismatic Catholic group. An American priest took me into a room to "pray over me". He "laid hands on me" but not in the usual healing style. It was terrifying. I was a troubled young woman heading for years in the psychiatric system. He certainly knew whom to pick!

Nine years ago I reported him to his religious order. To my horror, they told me he'd been in a treatment centre twice already to learn to "modify his ministry." He wrote to tell me "he'd learned to shut the gates"!

The religious order ignored my complaints, so I went to the police. The priest faced a three-hour interview; but, as there were no witnesses to my abuse as well as its being long ago, no case resulted. He, with the backing of the Marianists, denied it all. I went to the Archbishop, who made many promises. He reneged on nearly all of them and, nine years later, nothing has happened. No one is the slightest bit interested.

During that time of challenge and finding my voice, my artwork was going very well. Funded by the Arts and Disability Forum in Belfast, I held an exhibition. But the artwork was to be my last. I developed a neuromuscular disorder, and I now use a wheelchair.

So I took up photography. I passed my driving test at age 54, gave up smoking (40-60 a day!), liberated myself from psychiatry and drugs, and decided to *live*.

What can I say that is helpful? Never give up seeking *justice*. Never give up seeking *fulfilment*. Creativity in any medium is so *good* for the soul. Write your story.

It may be a long road, but I hope you find pure joy in nature. God gave us this beautiful earth. A slow walk by the sea at dawn with my two dogs makes me feel happy to be alive.

15

Bathsheba's Voice

Valli Boobal Batchelor

My dance choreography of a controversial biblical story entitled *Bathsheba's Voice* was premiered at the 42nd International Choreographers Showcase of Edinburgh Festival Fringe.

A review from the British Theater Guide noted that "Valli Batchelor's *Bathsheba's Voice* uses Australian and Indian dance forms to tell the biblical story of Bathsheba as a metaphor for violence against women. There are arresting moments, such as Bathsheba's seduction by David, which here is portrayed as rape."

Based on audience feedback, the performance appeared to have challenged many minds (including my own) under the creative and safe zone of artistic expression. David was Bathsheba's king and in a position to command. Bathsheba was another man's wife and in no position to resist.

The choreography was inspired by the UN's White Ribbon pledge "not to commit, condone or remain silent on violence against women and children" and is dedicated to the reclaimed voices of Australian victims of clergy sexual abuse. It explores a biblical story on the sexual violence and subsequent cover up by King David against Bathsheba, his loyal soldier's wife. It symbolizes the reclaimed voices of violated survivors of gender-based violence by spiritual leaders in churches. The choreography draws from traditional dance forms yet allows freedom from the constrictions of techniques to enable the expression of experiences. It consists of intricate steps in varying speeds and rhythmic measures of various counts. The dancers portrayal of emotions are communicated through the slower tempo and high melodic vocals of Rasa [experience] and Bhava [expression] adapted from the south Indian Bharata Natyam classical dance style.

As a trained classical Indian dancer, it was natural for me to express myself in this medium. Through many interactive workshops and dance presentations with survivors of violence, I have found that the dance medium is both expressive of the emotional hurts and needs of violated women and children as well as being cathartic and liberating for the individual in participation in group dramatic dance. The dance therefore becomes both the message of preventing violence as well as the medium of healing those who have been violated or who can empathize with them.

The acts of committing, condoning and/or remaining silent about sexual violence within churches are contemporary issues and should no longer be ignored. I attended a conference entitled "Sexual Abuse in Religious Context" at the University of New South Wales, Australia, and noted that the devastating effects from such betrayal of trust is a huge and immeasurable cost to Australians and churches worldwide.

As a believer in Jesus, I appeal to churches to hear the voices of clergy sexual abuse survivors, and work with experts, advocates and secular groups and to lobby decision-makers for the necessary changes that will create safer places of worship and healing for vulnerable members of the public who choose to attend churches.

16

When the Abuser Is a Husband

Victor Kaonga

Clergy are given respect in many parts of the world. But for 45-year Alinane (not her real name) in Malawi, her husband, a pastor in a Pentecostal charismatic church, was not deserving of any respect. She decided to speak out on how she survived abuse by her own husband, in spite of the fear of being misunderstood, of being seen as looking for sympathy, of drawing attention to herself and fear of being seen as aiming to destroy the church pastor. Journalist Victor Kaonga interviews Alinane on the abuse and how she survived the seven years in marriage.

How Did It Start?

I was married and had two girls. Unfortunately my husband passed away. In 2000, I married again, this time to a minister whose wife had passed away earlier. He had three children. My husband started giving preferential treatment to his children, which made things a bit tough for me. In addition, he was very fond of his mother and he would frequently visit his mother, who lived in another town.

In June 2002, we moved to the United States, where my husband was in school. I worked and paid for his tuition and our living. While there, we began not getting along. Whenever he had some money, he would simply send it home to his mother in Malawi. Or at least he claimed to do so. Even the hosts, students and fellow church members noted the growing bad practice.

Returning to Malawi in December 2006, we started a new ministry with support from persons we had met at church in the United States. Later my husband began benefiting from everything that was being sent to this church. He did this in spite of being a pastor at a church in Malawi's capital city of Lilongwe. I argued with him over this because I wanted us to be faithful with what Lord had provided for this ministry.

One day he beat me in the presence of his mother, who was visiting. Knowing that he was a pastor, the neighbors watched and laughed at us. It was an embarrassing moment for me.

What Followed Such Behavior?

Even if we slept in the same bed, he could go for two full weeks without uttering any word to me. At church on Sundays, he would say in the pulpit, "In my earlier marriage, we used to love each other a lot." Some people believed I am was the one who created conflicts. I was left without money. I started making small cakes to raise money.

He eventually took a lot of trips away from home. This affected his ministry and the elders became worried about his behavor. I heard that he was going out with other women. I was emotionally and physically abused. The police arrested him for abusing me just before we separated in March 2008.

How Did You Handle All This?

It was a tough time. While there were relatives who supported me. It was not easy. I needed sleeping pills for three months. I was angry and bitter at him. Imagine. I am a registered nurse, yet he had prevented me from working. Because of his behavior, I lost trust in the men of God. I even moved away from his church and started worshipping elsewhere. I wanted to destroy him. It was painful for me to hear that he was going to get married to someone else in that church. What shocked me most was that the woman he married was the same woman who been serving as an usherette at our earlier church in another city. And it now became clear that their relationship had started years earlier and well before our separation. Now I understood why he did not bother about our bedroom life and left the house frequently on the pretext that he was visiting his mother.

Did He Ever Abuse You Sexually?

(Silence). Uh no. But many times in a month he slept on the couch and not in the bedroom.

You Were Married to Him for Seven Years. Did You Have Children Together?

Apart from the fact we already had five children, I read the signs of the marriage early. Because of that, I decided the first year that I was not going to commit myself to having a child with him for fear that we would fail to take proper care of the child. But I also did not want a child who would be a constant reminder of him. This was a home where no week passed in seven years without a conflict.

You Have Survived Many Abuses. How?

God has been faithful to me. Frankly speaking, I can say something now. I forgave my husband and I had to let the experience go. I turned to the Bible over and over. As I read, I learned that vengeance is not mine but God's. I will let God fight my battle. I have certainly been bitter and I have wanted to destroy my former husband. I especially felt this way later on, when he married someone else. I made myself busy at church. I had to let it go.

Are You Aware of Any Women Who May Be in Situations Like Yours?

There are many women who have been sexually abused by men of God, but we do not like coming out in the open. We talk among ourselves. I know of a young girl who was impregnated by a pastor who was her own father. There are many cases of pastors exploiting women in their churches. My own aunt was abused sexually by her pastor. But who would want to disclose this? No one.

What Advice Do You Have for Fellow Women Abused by the Clergy?

Know that there is light at the end of the tunnel. Have hope. Pray for the abuser. Don't deny the problem. Don't demonise him. If married, identify some of his strengths. Be courageous and come out in the open. Speak out about the problem. Though it is not easy, share your story with others. Seek counsel and advice. I would encourage people around you to support you and identify with you.

Last Word

It was not easy. I thank God for healing my heart. He saw me in my darkest hour. I thank God for all who were there for me. And thank you for letting me share this with you. This speaking has been healing.

17

You Knew

Samantha Nelson

Full of hope and love for the Lord, they went to church that day.
They'd never guess the thoughts you had,
And that you'd one day lead them astray.
But you knew.

A husband longing for reassurance, a wife seeking to follow Him.
Newly returning to the faith,
They never suspected what you saw in them,
But you knew.

A woman naïve and trusting,
Too trusting for her good,
She wouldn't know what thoughts you had, perhaps she never would.
But you knew.

The husband trusted implicitly, he needed a mentor and a friend.
She looked for a loving father figure, a family to be in.
They thought you were a Godly man and wouldn't question otherwise,
But you knew.

Slowly you gained their trust and love,
It was a friendship they grew to cherish.
Your real motive was hidden to them,
But you knew.

As you gleaned their secrets,
And discovered their inner pain,
You sought to divide and conquer—at first they suspected nothing.
But you knew.

As your professed concern increased,
Their walls came tumbling down.
She gave you all her secrets not realizing her vulnerability.

But you knew.

The husband continued to trust, although it was not without doubt.
Your actions began to seem strange,
And he wondered, was this friendship or something else?
But you knew.

It was not a friendship that you intended, when you "set your sights"
on her.
They were blinded by your title, fooled by your bold nerve.
Where this would lead, they had not a clue,
But you knew.

You knew the path you were leading them, as you had been there
before.
Sure you've denied it, but truth speaks louder than words.
Your own wife couldn't stop you, she was in the dark.
But you knew.

Lives now ruined and in great pain,
The woman's hope all gone—the husband's nearly so.
With faith destroyed and love in pieces, they didn't know what you'd do.
But you knew.

How could you take her guilt and shame from years of past abuse,
Take her trusting, gentle heart and put it through such pain?
She believed and trusted in you, she thought it was safe to do.
But you knew.

How could you wrench her heart from the one she loved so dear?
How could you try to steal away the man God had given her?
She could not fathom what had changed—in her mind she was con-
fused.
But you knew.

She had come hoping to lead others to Christ.
Her husband felt the same.
The plans you laid were far and wide and unbeknownst to them.
But you knew.

Was it "counseling" when you forced yourself on her,
Telling her "just once"?
What could she do? You were in control.
But you knew.

Secrets kept are secret shame. Her life came crashing in.

No longer could this lie be hid,
You'd gone too far again.
But you knew.
    Her husband valiant at her side, thank God for his resolve.
He hoped he'd live to see her heal, and their marriage be renewed.
He didn't know what would come next,
But you knew.
    Stealthily and cunningly, like the cruelest foe,
You led them to a place of sin where life appeared to be no more.
The depth of evil in your heart, they'd never ever known,
But you knew.
    Only God could save them now and wrench her from your grasp.
It was a battle long and hard, for Satan was pleased with the catch.
If only they'd known your inner heart, the blackness residing there…
But you knew.
    With death so near the door, you simply refused to let go.
What would it take—a suicide—to make you let her go?
You vowed you'd never leave her, she didn't know what that meant.
But you knew.
    Your stalking has continued for many a year since,
You think they do not realize that it is your presence.
It's not your presence merely though, for Satan is leading you.
But you knew.
    You threw your life away, your family and career.
Did not God's call mean anything, were you too involved with you?
The devil had his way with you, and through you, others too.
But you knew.
    They wondered how many others you'd left lying in the dust.
How many broken hearts and lives, trampled in your path?
They knew they weren't the only ones…how many who could know?
But you knew.
    Have you seen the light of truth—that Jesus has died for you?

Have you given your life to Him and repented for what you've done?
They'll never know where you stand with Him,
But you know.

This life you live is not a game—there's more to life than sex and power.
By God's grace they pity you and pray for your salvation.
Will you seek your Lord and Savior—at this, the very last hour?
Only you know.

Part Three

Churches Addressing Clergy Misconduct

18

Step Forward in Faith

LORI MCPHERSON

Pastors and church leaders are often loathe to broach the topics of sexual abuse, domestic violence, sexual harassment and such related evils with their congregations. Quite honestly, we may avoid these conversations as we would the dreaded "birds and the bees talk" with our children! The reluctance to engage these subjects is understandable—they can be awkward, uncomfortable, and difficult to discuss. Many church leaders are ill-equipped to take on the challenge of doing so. Others may not even understand why having these "tough talks" are *so* critical to the well-being of their congregation.

As I navigate this brief essay, I want to take as our guide the prayer of Jesus for his disciples:

> All mine are yours, and yours are mine; and I have been glorified in them.
> And now I am no longer in the world, but they are in the world, and I am
> coming to you. Holy Father, protect them in your name that you have given
> me, so that they may be one, as we are one (John, 17:10-11 NRSV).

Just as Jesus asked God to protect his disciples, we are called to protect those in our congregations and communities from harm. That harm may come in the form of emotional, physical, sexual, or spiritual abuse, and we must not only be prepared to prevent harm where we are able, but also provide care for those who have been harmed.

Why is it so important that clergy and church leaders have the motivation and ability to care and protect in the ways described above? It is widely accepted that sexual abuse of women and children is endemic in the United States—anywhere from one-quarter to one-third (and often more, depending on the survey instrument) of Americans suffered some kind of sexual abuse, creating longlasting scars of every kind. These scars will need to be healed as part of a growing relationship with God.

The prevalence of sexual assaults of adults and domestic violence is also higher than we might expect, and at least some of our congregants are likely to have had such experiences. In addition, because of the inherent power imbalance between clergy and congregant, female parishioners will sometimes find themselves the victims of sexual harassment at the hands of their pastors.

The basic dynamics of abuse—whether perpetrated against a child or an adult—are similar. Abusers look for vulnerable victims. That vulnerability may take the form of the young age of a child, the lack of supervision of a "troubled" teenager, a developmentally delayed person, or a woman with few independent resources who seeks the kind ear of her pastor. To be clear, vulnerability is not a *cause* of an abuser's behavior! Regardless of how small, young, or dependent we are, *no one* has a right to abuse us, in any way.

As we provide pastoral care to those who have suffered from these abuses, we must take care to not cause further harm in our actions. For example, imagine a victim of child sexual abuse makes an appointment to see you and says that he had been struggling with forgiving his abuser. The easy, soft, spiritual answer would be to counsel towards forgiveness, that "Jesus commands us to forgive." To the ears of the person who has been abused, though, a command to forgive— from Jesus, through you as a person wearing the clerical collar—will often ignore the reality of their pain, fear, and justified anger over their abuse. Such counsel could whitewash the places where internal healing needs to be done, and could drive them further from God, rather than closer. Imagine, also, the loneliness and isolation of the divorcee who is being sexually harassed by the senior pastor and is faced with an untenable choice: to either remove herself and her children from the most stable community in their lives, or go without pastoral care—as she slowly loses her faith in the church—or even God. How do we develop the skills and resources to best provide pastoral care in the first example? How do we detect and prevent the sexual harassment by the pastor in the second example, while spiritually tending to the divorcee?

How can we meet our congregants—who know the experience of abuse first-hand—where they are, provide the care they need, and help them grow closer to God in the process? First, we must remember the old maxim "physician, heal thyself." Given the prevalence rates mentioned above, it comes as no surprise that countless clergy and church leaders have also experienced, or are still experiencing, sexual or physical abuse. Unfortunately, some also have perpetrated, or are still perpetrating, such abuse.

We must tend to ourselves, first. If we need to work through our own experiences of being abused, we must take the responsibility of seeking out that help. If we are continuing to abuse others, we must stop, and seek the help we need to stay stopped. Until our own house is in order such that we can provide pastoral care on these issues, we must have the courage and integrity to refer people out to our colleagues.

Next, we must be trained. Most of us will get through seminary without even having spent one class session discussing domestic and sexual violence or child abuse. This is a tremendous institutional gap, yes, and one I continue to work towards closing. Regardless of our seminary training or lack thereof, we must seek out the education we will need to best provide care. We can and should take advantage of community educational opportunities: mandatory reporter training from our child protection agencies, domestic violence training from a victims' advocacy organization, sexual harassment training from a diversity consultant, and the like. We can seek out books, articles, and experts available for consultation on professional ethics (particularly conflicts of interest in pastoral care) and boundary setting. My ministry in this field is focused on providing just these kinds of resources and training, and all are invited to contact me for assistance.

Pastoral care is part and parcel of what our obligation is to our communities, to be sure, but we are also called to provide a safe place where that care might take place. A church where it is publicly known that abuse—of any kind—will not be tolerated is a place where a victim will feel safer, and a potential abuser could even be deterred from engaging in predatory conduct at the church. To that end, many churches have adopted policies addressing sexual harassment and child protection in the church. The United Church of Christ has compiled a wonderful library of materials that is available online.

As clergy and church leaders we do not have the luxury of treating the reality of sexual abuse and domestic violence as things that are somehow foreign to the lives of our congregations. The painful truth is that the tapestry of our world is speckled with threads of abuse which can either form a basis for uniting in our healing—or dividing in our brokenness.

I want to close with the story from my days as a trial attorney. A stepfather had been accused, and was ultimately convicted of, repeatedly raping his young step-daughter. Prior to his arrest and incarceration, the family had been very involved in a local church community. What happened during every court hearing, though, was heartbreaking: the pastor showed up, every time, in support of the step-father. He did not seek to comfort the young step-daughter or her mother, and the church provided her no public support. Every time she was in that courtroom she was alone again, just as she had been alone every time her stepfather raped her. That pastor did untold spiritual damage to the young girl, by standing as a representative of God—and clearly on the side of the man who had done such horrible things to her. She deserved better. Every victim of abuse deserves better than this.

We are called to step forward in faith, meet the people where they are, and walk with them as they develop a deeper relationship with God. We are called to have courage and faith, enough to engage the difficult conversations and do the often-times excruciating work that will lead to healing for us, and our congregants. To do any less is to ignore Jesus' prayer, and our call: to protect those in our charge.

19

Self-Questioning from the Caribbean

Nicqui Ashwood

Clergy sexual misconduct continues to be a troubling issue in the Caribbean region and in Jamaica in particular. There have been at least three cases of ministerial sexual abuse which have made the headlines in the Jamaican papers last two years—two taking place on local soil and the other involving a Jamaican minister overseas. The public responses to these incidents are varied, especially in relation to other "newsworthy" items that seem to cloud or overshadow these, causing them to pale in comparison. That they have been overshadowed does not make them less bothersome; for one is aware that for every crime which is reported, there are several others which gain less prominence. And the problem will only persist if we as clergy and laity remain silent.

It is possible that *fear* remains one of the key reasons behind most churches' and denominations' silence about sexual misconduct in the church. Fear of dealing with the issue of sexuality on the whole and, further, dealing with clergy or diaconal sexual misconduct. Perhaps it is that we are concerned that if we speak to such matters, our own human frailties will come to the fore—"Remove my own log before attempting to address my neighbors's specks."

The response to sexuality in the region seems to be linked to a distorted Augustinian response to the sex act. For it is purported that Augustine, upon conversion, portrayed sex as evil and saw it as a primary trigger for sin. This is compounded by the vestiges of slavery, which perpetuated the belief that persons of African ancestry were beasts and basal or primitive in our sexual activities and relationships. In several contexts, the Levitical[1] principles are cited as the grounds for reprimanding a young lady who has been found "guilty" of sexual misconduct. Unfortunately, there are few laws recorded in the canon that speak to managing sexuality and responding to the perpetrators of such acts, and therein lies the crux of the matter.

As a female who has had to relate to victims of clergy abuse, I find that it is not so easy to seek recourse in the biblical texts. Those texts[2] place the blame on the woman, who seems to invite abuse simply by being female and tempting. In many parts of the biblical canon, females are categorized as either harlots or princesses,[3] and once her virtue is taken, she has no recourse from moral society.

Further, I do not see the matter of abuse as one which may only be addressed from the perspective of silence. For, in my mind, clergy abuse—like most other acts of abuse—reflects internalized psychosocial responses of the abuser to power vested in him or her. It is thus not only the victim who is in need of resuscitation, but also the perpetrator.

A Man like That

Please join me in a moment of retrospection—to my initial response to hearing a devastating story of clergy sexual abuse. She was graphic, leaving little to the imagination. She was hurt—by the pain of the retelling as well as the pain of betrayal, which still cut to the core of her spirituality. She was violated, by one whom she trusted, confided in, respected, held in high regard. She was not his first victim.

I was livid. "How could he?" I thought to myself, "A man like that should be drawn and quartered, castrated, or at least locked up permanently for abuse of his status, his authority, his power! A man like that . . ." I paused in my mental diatribe as the real complexity of it all struck to the core of *my* being. For *'a man like that'* could very easily have been me. I really wished in those moments of ranting that I could have held myself up as a paragon of virtue to say that all clergy should be just like me, but I too have fallen prey to the sin of abuse of status, authority and power.

As a clergy woman, I too battle daily the siren song which seeks to call me away from the vows I made before God and the wider community. *My* vows included a solemn promise: to tend the flock of God committed to their care, not by constraint but willingly, not for selfish gain but eagerly, not by domineering over those in their charge but by example. I pledged to care for the people of God: nourishing, teaching, and encouraging them; giving direction to the life of the congregation;counseling the troubled; declaring God's forgiveness of sin; and proclaiming victory over death. I have tried valiantly to keep this promise. But when the impact of my authority and responsibilities are coupled with the stresses of life, I sometimes lose control, and displaced aggression is my "natural" recourse" (cf. Kathleen McGowan, 2005).

Granted, I have not been guilty of sexually abusing or assaulting my parishioners. But, in many instances, when a clergyperson is stretched, it is sometimes translated in sexual terms. Further, it has been argued that a variation of the practice of *droit de seigneur* is still acceptable for persons in power, including members of the clergy (cf. Liz Kelly, 1996). How easy it becomes for us as clergy to become misguided, abusing the power and authority invested in us!

Her words gripped me again, as she described her feelings of self-revulsion, scorn and shame at the ministrations of her abuser; feelings which later morphed into a sense of powerlessness and abandonment. Perhaps it was her sense of abandonment which again struck a nerve and caught my attention; because she said that the first person whom she felt had abandoned her was God! I wanted to shout, "No! That is not true, God is *with* you, truly suffering alongside you; you are not alone!" She turned and fixed her vacant eyes on me when she declared,

> I know God abandoned me, because it was God's messenger who assaulted me and remains at large because people, including other members of the clergy, are silent! Tell me, where is this God that you all speak of, who gives priority to the poor, the oppressed, and metes out justice to wrongdoers?

I realized that it was not just the clergy who were on trial here, but God's own self. But, while God will stand trial, God also remains an arbiter of justice. I thought of characters in the Hebrew Bible who represented God at the highest levels, who were guilty of similar crimes of passion: Abraham and David. Abraham sentenced his wife into prostitution *twice*, so that he might escape "sure and certain" death (albeit because of the beauty of the very same wife). He compounded that act of domination and power by agreeing to his wife's demands that he copulate with his servant—Hagar –that he might fulfill God's will. *Power corrupts.* Abraham's actions were tantamount to Jim Jones's many acts of clergy abuse, which led to the mass suicide in Guyana in the 1980s. And yet Abraham was a friend of God and a Hall of Faith-er (Heb. 11:8-12).

Having spent many years learning and leaning at the king's feet, David *knew* what it meant to be a ruler of integrity. As one who spent even more years hiding from the very same king in order that God's will might be accomplished, David knew firsthand the perils and extremities of abuse of power. And, lured by the Bathsheba's beauty, David succumbed and fell prey to abuse of power. He saw Bathsheba, slept with her, and murdered her husband to cover his infidelity (2 Sam 11–12). *Absolute power corrupts absolutely.* But neither David, nor Abraham, nor the clergypersons who have abused our calling are in actual possession of absolute power. God is not mocked, not even by those whom God has chosen as emissaries and representatives.

For both Abraham and David had to deal with God's law. Abraham, through Ishma'el and Isaac, is considered the father of Judaism and Islam. The enmity between those peoples remains a painful reality in Middle Eastern states today. David's family was embroiled in the most embarrassing saga of rivalry and revenge, which led eventually to the division of the kingdom. When members of the clergy abuse our power, our spiritual lives disintegrate, and our actions—if unchecked—set in motion a spiral of events which negatively affect our physical and spiritual families. But most of all, it splits congregations and leads to the general malaise with and apathy toward the church at large.

Truth, Healing, and Hope

Undoubtedly, when a clergyperson sins, there *are* repercussions. And it is incumbent upon all God's anointed to ensure that when power corrupts, the root of the corruption be annihilated absolutely. The accused *must* be removed from that context immediately. The rest of us are called to a ministry of healing and reconciliation –toward both perpetrator and victim (and their families). We are called to restore the abused person's sense of self in positive uplifting ways that assure them of God's presence with them and healing power. This may be realized through counseling, confession and a request for forgiveness, not by ignoring the sin in the hope that it will disappear. We *must* name the sins of abuse for what they are. And we are called—in God's love—to allow justice to prevail *uncompromisingly.* For it is in the true exercise of justice that those who have suffered from clergy abuse may once again find peace with God.

Jesus' earthly ministry offered healing to all who desired it. We have a responsibility to create spaces where—eventually—both the abused and the abuser are able to congregate with all the rest of us fallen saints, finding healing in Christ, assured in the knowledge that in Christ we are new creations, the old is past, and we become peacemakers and restorers of the breach. This invites us to become agents of transformation, offering spaces for confession, testimony, and openness. As church, we must give voice to the silenced, shifting the balance of power from the powerful to the victimized, assuring them that they will not be further punished for someone else's wrongs.

This may come through special healing services for victims and then for victimizers. Our counselors should be trained to recognize the signs and to act on them. Psychological testing is important, but so too is counseling and removal when abuse is proven. We need to identify and birth programmes that help the offenders to name and claim and in turn desist from their acts of abuse of power. The church must break the silence on sexual abuse—within and without. For when the silence is broken, healing, and wholeness replaces brokenness, anger, abuse and despair. Hope is restored and the church once again calls others into the fullness of abundant life offered to us all through Christ Jesus.

Will you join me in providing that message of hope?

20

Women in the Congo

ESTHER LUBUNGA KENGE

s it the end of the world? When unusual things happen, when incredible stories are being told, Christians think of the Last Days, the Apocalypse that will put an end to our earthly life. In the eastern part of Congo, the unusual things were started by the six-year war that followed the genocide in Rwanda and Burundi on the other bank of the African Great Lakes region. This conflict was quickly transformed into a civil war on the side of the Democratic Republic of Congo that lasted from 1996 to 2002, creating a situation of insecurity that will take long to be removed.

The aftermath of this war is even more devastating than the killing that took place during the war. Women and girls are being raped daily by various groups of armed people. Victims of rape face the danger of not only being infected by the HIV virus, but also by being discriminated and rejected by spouses and family members. In the past, victims of human violence and oppression would find solace in the church, considered as the haven of peace.

What is strange today is that the church is no longer a secure hiding place, and ministers of God are no longer always good shepherds of the flock. Most of them confirming the word of the gospel are wolves wearing the skin of a lamb. I know of a number of ministers in our church who are today under discipline. Most of them are accused of taking advantage of widows in the church. In a country destroyed by the war and in which most of people are jobless, the situation of widows without skill is very bad. Most of them are being helped by church members for survival. The strange phenomenon is that several cases of sexual abuse are reported in various denominations involving the clergy and powerless widows and girls. We know that not all women would be courageous enough to denounce publicly a servant of God. Many would prefer to keep the secret to their death instead of bringing disgrace to a person who is leading the church of God. Recently it was a case of a thirteen year-old daughter of a widow appeared before the Church Council because she was found pregnant. She acknowledged that during the night she saw the pastor taking advantage of her, but she took it to be a bad dream until the day she realized that she was pregnant. Poor girl, she has fallen into the trap of a perpetrator who pretended to be her protector. She was so naïve that although she knew that she was being raped, she refused to believe the reality, as it was beyond what she could bear, so much so that she resolved to take it as a dream. But the reality cannot be hidden forever.

As I think of this situation, I wonder what has gone wrong with the clergy. On the one hand, people think the church as a whole is experiencing decay by the decline of spirituality and morality that affects even the clergy. On the other hand, this is not a new phenomenon. Some clergy—both women and men—have always indulged themselves in this practice but were covered by the immunity that people gave them. It was taboo to speak out about vices committed by clergy. As people suffer, they reach a point that they cannot take it any more. They are obliged to go public with their story. Women, more than ever before, are being taught by many organizations about their rights. Even when they are powerless before the perpetrators, they should be bold to speak out and speak loud. Now that many women are taking seriously lessons from various seminars and workshops, one can predict that the hidden sins of the clergy, especially those related to sexual abuse of women, will be more and more exposed to the light.

It is not the end of the world but the beginning of a new era in which everything that is done in secret should be brought to light. Those who were hiding behind the silence of the victims should face the exposure of their actions to the public. Thank God that not all the clergymen are rapists. God has genuine shepherds of the flock ready to sacrifice their lives for the sheep.

21

Breaking the Silence in Thailand

Janejinda Pawadee

Violence against women is a manifestation of historically unequal power relations between men and women, which leads to domination and discrimination against women. It is one of the crucial issues by which women are forced into subordinate positions as compared to men.

According to Article 1 of the UN Declaration on the Elimination of Violence against Women, the phrase *violence against women* means "any act of gender-based violence that results in, or is likely to result in, physical, sexual or psychological harm or suffering to women, including threats of such acts, coercion or arbitrary deprivation of liberty, whether occurring in public or in private life."

This declaration urges that the rights of women and girls are an inalienable, integral and indivisible part of universal human rights, and there is a need to further promote and protect them.

Being a Victim of Violence

As a woman, I often experienced and suffered from violence, including sexual abuse and sexual harassment. When I was only eight years old, my uncle touched my breast, but I was too young to learn that it was sexual abuse. I did not dare to tell my parents because I was afraid they would beat me up and I would be accused of making up a story against my uncle.

When I was a university student, I faced an attempted rape by one of my senior friends, who continued his master's studies in divinity and is now serving as a church pastor. In another incident, I experienced sexual harassment by an elder of a famous church in Chiang Mai, who asked me to sleep with him when I was alone in my apartment.

When violence happens, it takes a lot of courage to speak out. Like any other victim of violence, I also had to be brave enough to speak about it. I had to explain to people that "it was not my fault." Fortunately, most of people who heard my stories believed me, despite the fact that talking about sexual abuse and harassment in our culture is taboo. It is often taken as merely a joke by the society, regardless of how painful it is for the ones who suffer this violence.

123

As an advocate for the rights of women and children for more than fifteen years, I have heard the stories of different kinds and experiences of violence. Most of the cases I heard about were related to sexual abuse and harassment. These happen in all situations and settings, including families and churches.

Some years ago, I was working for the case of one girl of twelve years who was raped by her village pastor and by an elder of church in the city where she was at boarding school. Both abusers were proved to be guilty and were sentenced to jail for different periods of time. The victim was so embarrassed to tell anyone because it happened in a church, and she was afraid that people would think that she had made up the story. During that time, the city church committee refused my interventions, arguing that "the church's reputation" would be damaged. I challenged the church, arguing that they should protect a victim and not an abuser. In fact, the reputation of Christianity is damaged when churches protect abusers rather than victims. In such situations it is important that churches are challenged to play their role rather than siding with the perpetrators of violence. The Christian teaching of protecting human rights and dignity is something churches need to show, along with their preaching.

There are many other stories I keep on hearing about female youth and women who were sexually abused by their church pastors. These victims are vulnerable and voiceless, and afraid to tell people, thinking that people will not believe that such things happen in the church. The fact is that these incidences do happen, but the voices of such women are not being heard for several reasons. One reason is that victims fear being stigmatized in the church community and the society, that that they will not be able to explain that it was not "their fault."

Churches have to be safe places for all, including women and children. Church leaders and congregational members must condemn all kinds of violence and should not let abuse happen in their communities. Churches need to work to make sure that in their congregations women and children are safe and that sexual violence is prevented.

A church pastor should be dismissed immediately from his position in the church once an act of sexual abuse is proved against him. The investigation against such perpetrators should be held without any bias, and the related criminal laws should be used against them to ensure justice is served. Churches should not keep silent about the sexual violence. They need to break the silence. The situation can be much worse if such violence can keep on happening again and again. Churches have to take it more seriously and should formulate a policy not to recruit a pastor who has a reputation of sexual abuse against women or children. Gender concerns and human rights are subjects that should be part of the curriculum in the seminaries. It has to be part of Christian education that students learn to respect all human beings and their rights, especially women and children.

International Day for the Elimination of Violence against Women

November 25 was declared the International Day for the Elimination of Violence against Women as a result of a United Nations resolution in 1999. The date itself commemorates the assassination of three Mirabal sisters from the Dominican Republic. They were constant critics of the dictatorship of Rafael Leónidas Trujillo, and they gave birth to a strong public movement against Trujillo's dictatorship.

This UN resolution involved governments, international organizations and non-governmental organizations in efforts to raise public awareness about the issue of violence against women and their rights. It has brought the world's attention to how violence against women is an obstacle in a way to achieve equality, development and peace. It has also highlighted the plight of groups of women, such as minorities, indigenous women, refugee women, migrant women, women living in rural or remote communities, destitute women, women in institutions or in detention, girls, women with disabilities, elderly women and women in situations of armed conflict, who are particularly vulnerable to violence. Violence against women needs to be remembered and should be worked on all year long—not only on 25 November.

Bringing an End to the Violence

Every Christmas season we are reminded of Jesus Christ's birth, which led to freedom and salvation. Yet as we sing the song "Silent Night, Holy Night," we ignore the "silenced voices" of women and children who are oppressed and abused within our churches.

Why should we not celebrate every day as if it were Christmas by aiming to free women and children in the church of Jesus from any form of violence? We could start by helping women and children to break their oppressing silence—by listening, believing and supporting them as we promote and protect their rights.

22

The Case of Thailand

KENNETH DOBSON

In Thailand the vast majority of ordained clergy of all religions are men, and as in other societies clergy are traditionally accorded higher status and held to higher standards than most other sectors of society. For example, the lowest ranking or youngest ordained Buddhist priest or novice ranks higher in official protocol than the highest member of the Royal Family. What this means is that any hint of misconduct must be avoided and the separation of Buddhist priests from all women is supposed to be rigidly adhered. The fact that Protestant clergy can be married is somewhat confusing to the wider society and lowers the status of clergy and the church a notch or two in their view. But Protestant clergy are still accorded high social status and expected to adhere to high standards of conduct. Clergy are expected to be married sooner or later and be role-models of Christian family values. This actually puts a great deal of pressure on clergy, and forces them to keep a respectable social distance from a lot of what is going on in their communities (some of which they probably should be involved with, such as social movements or community development). Clergy and their families begin to feel they have no privacy or freedom, and the stress on clergy children in particular is immense. This is the first contextual factor in Thailand: clergy are deeply inhibited by the constant vigilance of society from all forms of sexual misconduct.

The second contextual factor is, in effect, just the opposite. Domestic and interpersonal matters are carefully respected in Thai society. The downside of this is that domestic violence is ignored, abuse is ignored, and everything that goes on inside the family is a family matter and is of no concern to anybody else. That is the prevailing point of view. Furthermore, monogamous values are not deeply rooted. For most of history, until the influence of European morality began to be felt, other social rules than the one-wife-one-husband rule applied. Romantic ideas of marriage held little attraction, for marriage was about maintaining society and romance was a side-show. The higher one's social status, the more this was true. People in the lower economic levels simply could not afford the luxuries of romance. Whereas, this is no longer as true as it was a century ago, the ideas about what constitutes sexual immorality are imprecise. This can contribute to license.

However, there is a third factor that is increasingly important and becoming better understood and more widely accepted. It has to do with human dignity and justice. Women are becoming more informed about their rights as human beings and more assertive. "We aren't going to take it anymore!" is increasingly heard and appreciated as a positive stance. Two factors work against this, one being that there is immense stigma against confrontation in this society, and the other being that women do hold immense subtle power in ways that anthropologists are just beginning to evaluate. It is clear and obvious, for example, that women are vastly under-represented in parliament and throughout the government. But, although that would be something of an intolerable state of affairs in some countries, here most people do not hold the government in high respect anyway, nor want to become involved. There are other ways that women exercise power in this society. This article cannot take time to short to document how women yield power, but any study would be flawed if it did not investigate the "mother factor." The military in Thailand may exercise the most political influence of any social institution, but if the goal is power why would one want to be a general if he could be the mother of a general? Thai society holds that mothers and teachers are the most influential agents for character formation and social control, and both those institutions are dominated by women. Women have other pervasive and subtle forms of power as well, and there is a consensus and contentment with this that it would be hard to change. Still, if men's exercise of power begins to infringe on that, women and their advocates are more likely to become re-assertive than they were over the past couple of centuries. And that brings us to the issue of sexual misconduct.

It is highly debatable, but I will not debate it here, that the definitions of "sexual misconduct" that are being developed in other parts of the world could achieve agreement by a majority here. On the other hand, here it would be misconduct for a Buddhist priest to touch the hand of a female of any age, whereas shaking hands is not thought of as either sexual or as misconduct in Europe or North America. What is misconduct, in other words, is a contextual matter. Insofar as sexual misconduct involves the misuse of the power inherent in one's very position as a clergy person to get a person of the opposite sex (in our discussion these being women) to yield to a suggestion that she would not otherwise be willing to assent to, then Thai clergy and parishioners would agree. Insofar as the layperson has the right to veto as well as to initiate any social activity what-soever, including any that are sexual, Thai people would agree. Thailand might possibly be toward the forefront of societies where even the possibility of a hint of impropriety between the sexes is to be avoided. So perhaps on the larger mat-ters there is a basis for joining in a general and global effort (such as this one) to minimize and eliminate sexual misconduct of clergy with women.

What is needed, in the Thai context, is something more basic, and possibly more important. The sexual empowerment of women in Thailand is thwarted to an extent that is greater than some other parts of the world by an inhibition or even a taboo, and certainly a vast confusion, concerning sex education and sexual health. There are periodic drives to promote sex education in schools, and the efforts are often watered down and limited to discussions of birds and bees. There is still a general feeling that "the more kids know about sex the more they will want to do it." It goes without saying that boys as well as girls are ignorant of how power, sex, love, and health are related and how they are best handled. Clergy and other adults are also harmed by misinformation and preju-dice. For instance, most Thai clergy would be unwilling to entertain the notion that a human being's sexuality is not a binary (either/or, male or female) matter, although Thailand has traditionally held that there are three sexes, males, females and "katoeys," who are females born in male bodies. As long as girls and young women are prevented from completely coming to full understanding of their being and nature, they will be disadvantaged, and withholding that knowledge is a form of abuse.

What is not needed here in Thailand is the continued importation and impo-sition of foreign cultural persuasions about sexual conduct. Thai social customs are strict enough to prevent erosion of human dignity and society. It is unneces-sary for missionaries, formerly from America and Europe, and now from other Asian countries, to tell Thai Christians how to behave. Colonialism, new and old, has never gone over well here in Thailand. On the other hand, Thailand can be a willing participant and valuable asset in a global discussion of the appropri-ate and inappropriate forms of sexual conduct, uses of power and authority, and expressions of Christian insight.

23

Creating a Response Team

Susan Jamison

My first experience with clergy sexual misconduct began in 1991, when I was asked to fill in for three weeks for a colleague who was on a family-in-crisis leave. I stayed there for eight months. The fifth month, after my a colleague surrendered his credentials, I learned that he had initiated a romantic affair with a member of the congregation. This information came not from the District Superintendent (DS) but from the woman involved, and only because she heard me talking about my plans to attend the first national training on Clergy Sexual Ethics. After listening to her story, I immediately called the District Superintendent and shared what I had learned, only to be told that the Cabinet and Bishop already knew.

I could scarcely contain my anger. The members of the congregation were blaming themselves, thinking they had caused their pastor to have a nervous breakdown. There was no Response Team to help this congregation. As a result of that experience, my Conference's first Clergy Sexual Ethics policy was written by our conference COSROW (Commission on the Status and Role of Women), which included the need for a Response Team. Soon the first Response Team members were named by the Bishop, and we held a training session to begin formulating a protocol. It took some time for the Bishop and Cabinet to learn how to utilize us.

Twenty years later, the Susquehanna Conference has a Response Team of 25 persons who have been trained to respond to congregations where misconduct has occurred or been alleged. We have a convener who coordinates cases and writes the official reports that are sent to the Bishop and Cabinet. The team is made up of a mixture of clergy and lay, men and women, who have a variety of skills and experience that has been critical to our success. The Response Team meets twice a year to review current cases, refine our process, recruit new members, decide what other training we need, and to have a safe place to talk about our own needs and feelings.

Over the years we have learned a great deal about the importance of:
- truth telling
- the power of an apology by a Cabinet representative for the harm that has been done
- the need for all parties concerned to have a trained advocate with whom they can talk and receive accurate information about the process
- the role of the Staff/Parish relations committee as leaders in the healing process
- the value of congregational meetings where folks can speak honestly about their feelings in small groups facilitated by Response Team members
- not taking it personally when we become targets for the anger of congregations
- patience in listening
- realizing that no two cases are exactly alike, although there are often similar elements
- the need for education about the abuse of power that is often at the root of the offending pastor's behavior

All those persons in the conference who are in a ministerial role, whether clergy or lay, must attend a Basic Boundaries Training within the first six months of being appointed or assigned to a parish. This training has been standardized and currently includes talking about what boundaries are, viewing a DVD containing vignettes that portray common situations in the church and then discussing them, the process which happens once a complaint is made, and information about how to establish healthy boundaries. Resources used include the DVD "Ask Before You Hug" made by the General Commission on the Status and Role of Women and distributed by EcuFilm, *Safe Connections: What Parishioners Can Do to Understand and Prevent Clergy Sexual Abuse* , produced by the Evangelical Lutheran Church in America Division for Ministry and published by Augsburg Fortress, and the current Sexual Ethics policy of the conference.

Twice we have had church members who have been through our process volunteer to share their story with churches that were just beginning the process, because they knew how valuable it was to have the Response Team in their midst. Now a call to the Response Team is one of the first things that happens when a credible allegation of misconduct occurs. Our ministry is one of healing and reconciliation, as well as a call for accountability. We know we make a positive difference in the Conference's ability to respond with compassion and justice, and that healing is possible.

24

Methodists React

SALLY DOLCH

Survey data and informal estimates suggest that there may be five hundred cases of clergy sexual misconduct in the United Methodist Church within the United States each year. Congregations encountering clergy misconduct experience grief and a disorienting sense of betrayal. Yet response teams can make the difference between a church that is wounded but able to heal and a church that is mortally damaged. Congregations in crisis and theological confusion due to misconduct need and deserve compassionate and empowering intervention to move through conflict to restoration.

In the United Methodist Church, the policies guiding response to clergy sexual misconduct are found in *The Book of Discipline* and *The Book of Resolutions*. They are updated every four years at General Conference. Authority for response to misconduct lies with conference episcopal leaders and response varies widely across conferences. At least five boards and agencies that sit at the United Methodist Connectional Table have identified roles related to sexual ethics in the church. Yet, understanding United Methodist and conference policies, resolutions, and leadership for sexual ethics is foundational to the development of training, protocols for response, and movement toward the denomination's goal of "eradication of sexual misconduct from the church."

Every conference response to clergy sexual misconduct is different and the majority of conferences do not have a clergy sexual misconduct response team. However, the underlying assumption herein is that a ministry of response to congregations is efficacious and a best practice for managing the fallout of clergy sexual misconduct and essential to the healing and well-being of congregations. This review of conference sexual ethics policies and surveys and interviews with response team conveners identified a large number of best practices that are making a difference in the lives of clergy misconduct victims and their fellow church members.

Leadership is required by judicatory officials to ensure that the conference has done everything possible to prevent clergy sexual misconduct and that protocols are in place when it happens. Every act of prevention, preparation, and

131

response is part of the intervention for the primary victim and the congregation. Episcopal or judicatory "best practices" for congregational health following
clergy sexual misconduct include :

(1) promoting honesty about the problem of clergy sexual misconduct
through adoption of clear, comprehensive conference sexual ethics policies that
identify a process for response, are updated every four years, and are made acces-
sible to clergy and laity;

(2) timely calling for a trained response team to guide healing for affected
congregations, while at the same time appropriately honoring confidentiality;

(3) taking time to build trust relationships with team conveners and congregations;

(4) fostering interim ministry through appointment of individuals gifted and
trained for the role of after pastor; and

(5) facilitating a support network for interim pastors.

In addition, open communication between judicatory leaders and laity
increases healing when:

(1) sexual ethics policies identify response teams and contact numbers for
reporting;

(2) policies and brochures are widely circulated to congregations on paper
such as newsletters and handouts, and on the web;

(3) sexual ethics training is provided for clergy and laity; and

(4) the bishop writes a disclosure letter to a congregation which is read publicly by a district superintendent and mailed to each member.

When deployed, response teams reflect passionate commitment and congregations display evidence of healing. The most effective response teams:

(1) are guided by an intervention manual;

(2) prioritize ongoing training and networks with other seasoned response
teams, as well as keeping up-to-date with the misconduct literature;

(3) seek membership based on diverse gifts, geography, passion for the work,
and reflect the congregations they will encounter;

(4) are small enough to simplify coordination, but large enough to accom-
modate multiple interventions without burning out team members;

(5) plan for multiple meetings per year to build skills and trust;

(6) plan for a debriefing after every intervention; and

(7) ensure accountability to and an ongoing relationship with the bishop
through frequent convener communication.

In addition, response teams that:

(1) share their knowledge as sexual ethics trainers for clergy and laity;

(2) seek to apply their intervention skills to other conflict resolution situations; and

(3) mentor interim ministers find that they: (a) increase their own knowledge; (b) and sustain their enthusiasm and spirit for the work; (c) keep team momentum between interventions; (d) build trust with peers and judicatory leaders; and (e) keep boundaries issues before the conference as a prevention strategy.

Congregational intervention "best practices" that help a congregation make the choice to heal include:

(1) responding quickly, preferably at the point of congregational disclosure;

(2) planning carefully for devotions considering the particulars of the trauma in each congregation;

(3) meeting with church leaders and the district superintendent or other judicatory leader prior to meeting the congregation;

(4) ensuring time for questions and sacred listening to each person in the congregation who needs to be heard and affirmed;

(5) having the district superintendent or judicatory representative read the disclosure letter and provide assurances about the future of the congregation;

(6) meeting with the congregation as often as they request and checking in with the congregation periodically after the initial disclosure meeting;

(7) guiding the congregation to theological reflection that assists healing; and

(8) offering a non-anxious presence to people experiencing great stress and upheaval.

Several additional practices not yet as widely practiced, but developed and implemented by individual response teams or judicatory leaders, include:

(1) innovative strategies for securing sexual ethics prevention training for team members such as collaboration with the conference insurance company, partnering with neighboring conferences to share training, or joining with other denominations to share resources;

(2) developing specialized training for Staff Parish Relations or church personnel committees to ensure that the members who are in the best position to head off a problem situation are knowledgeable and informed;

(3) developing evaluation strategies to assess impact of the intervention such as written surveys for all who attend disclosure or congregational response meetings or follow-up telephone interviews with church leaders to assess healing; and

(4) changing fitness and competence criteria for all clergy candidates before they are appointed or hired to ensure that those at greater risk for boundary violations address those risk factors prior to entering the ministry.

The experience of practicing United Methodist response teams committed to prevention and compassionate intervention will continue to teach us about healing possibilities for congregations because deployment of theologically grounded response teams is essential for healing congregations who have experienced clergy sexual misconduct.

Selected Bibliography

Chaves, Mark, and Garland, Diana. "The Prevalence of Clergy Sexual Advances toward Adults in Their Congregations." *Journal of the Scientific Study of Religion* (48) 4, 817–24. *www.baylor.edu/clergysexualmisconduct/*

Evinger, James S. *Annotated Bibliography of Clergy Sexual Abuse, 15th revision.* Rochester, New York: 2008. www.faithtrustinstitute.org.

Fortune, Marie M. *Is Nothing Sacred? The Story of a Pastor, the Women He Sexually Abused, and the Congregation He Nearly Destroyed.* Cleveland: United Church Press, 1999. Originally published by Harper San Francisco, 1989.

Gaede, Beth Ann, ed. *When a Congregation Is Betrayed, Responding to Clergy Misconduct.* Washington, DC: Alban Institute, 2006.

Hopkins, Nancy Myer, and Mark Laaser, eds. *Restoring the Soul of a Church: Healing Congregations Wounded by Clergy Sexual Misconduct.* Collegeville: Liturgical, 1995.

Kornfeld, Margaret. *Cultivating Wholeness: A Guide to Care and Counseling in Faith Communities.* New York: Continuum, 2000.

MacDonald, Bonnie. "Responding to Clergy Sexual Misconduct: Facilitating Congregational Healing and Restoration." DMin project paper, Louisville Presbyterian Theological Seminary, 2007.

Neinaber, Susan. "Leading into the Promised Land: Lessons Learned from Resilient Congregations. Herndon: Alban Institute, Summer 2006, Number 3.

Olesen, Harriett Jane, ed. *The Book of Discipline of the United Methodist Church 2008.* Nashville: United Methodist Publishing, 2008.

———, ed. *The Book of Resolutions of the United Methodist Church 2008.* Nashville: United Methodist Publishing, 2008.

Ruth, Kibbie Simmons, and Karen A. McClintock. *Healthy Disclosure: Solving Communication Quandaries in Congregations.* Herndon: Alban Institute, 2007.

Shupe, Anson, William A. Stacey, Susan E. Darnell, eds. *Clergy Misconduct in Modern America: Bad Pastors.* New York: New York University Press, 2000.

25

A Theological Framework

GARRY PRIOR

Experience with church governance across denominations has convinced me that, beyond secular standards, basic guidelines for religious professionals need to be established which, however old-fashioned, are rooted in a traditional understanding of the nature of sin. The greatest aphrodisiac is opportunity.

Establishing Inviolable Boundaries

Anyone in a position of religious leadership and trust is vulnerable to sexual misconduct. In any relationship where there is a deep bond of respect or gratitude between people of opposite sexes, there is the potential for sin. Spiritual leaders need to guard against it prudentially. In a close emotional environment, for example in a cross-gender counselling session, the very success of the session may generate the feelings of closeness that can so easily turn into temptation and indulgence. How the pastor or leader responds will determine the course of the relationship and possibly the future character of the pastor or leader.

It is quite natural for a grateful woman, for example, to embrace a man who has helped her. In today's churches, there is a lot of physical demonstration of affection. It only takes a moment to go too far. Sexual attraction is not a sin. Sexual arousal is not a sin. Sexual action is a sin, and it is up to the pastor or leader to avoid or even escape the situation where he can be put to the test (Proverbs 16:2, 16). If an emotionally needy pastor or leader feels gratification from the admiration and gratitude that his input has generated, then it is terribly easy to go too far. If by word or action, the desire is made known, it may either be received gratefully, with indignation or in confusion. None are good for the relationship or the counselling.

If received gratefully, the woman may feel valued, and it may seem such a simple way to demonstrate gratitude and closeness. Mary Magdalene's song in "Jesus Christ Superstar" poignantly explores the dilemma in "I don't know how to love him." It may "feel so right; but it is always wrong (Exodus 20:14). For a pastor or leader who experiences this for the first time, the action he takes may determine a future course of action. If he succumbs to the temptation, he may be horrified. Or he may feel that he has discovered a way to satisfy his desires. In the first case, the offender is a situational failure. In the second case, the offender may have started on a predatory course of abusing vulnerable women in his sphere of influence. (For a helpful analysis, see Roy Bell and Stanley Grenz, *Betrayal of Trust: Sexual Misconduct In the Pastorate* [Downers Grove: Intervarsity. 1995]). Both are offenders and must be dealt with. The standard of expected conduct is much higher for ordained than nonordained leaders (Luke 12:48 and 1 Timothy 5:7). Both have transgressed and bring dishonour on their calling.

For the victim, and that is the right word (even where, as sometimes happens, the woman is the initiator), there must be strict barriers to protect her. The taboos must be very clear and understood. Preferably, the taboos should be known to both sides, but at the very least the pastor or leader should be extremely conscious of them.

Guidelines

Good guidelines are obvious but not always perceived. For example, do not ask a man to counsel a woman one-on-one and vice versa. Even if there is no impropriety, it is always possible for a misunderstanding to occur. I once arranged for a counselling to take place based on race. The man and the woman, both single, were of the same race. A hurt woman perceived the counselling mission as a romantic initiative and was reportedly devastated when that turned out not to be the case.

Leaders should avoid situations in which propriety may be offended, for example, being alone in a room with a woman with no other woman in proximity. Third parties might misconstrue (James 3:6-7). Pastoral visits should not be one-on-one where the sexes are different. Home visits when the person is alone should be avoided unless one is accompanied. Teams help avoid problems.

The Asian values of not touching across the sexes may seem quaint in today's "touchy-feely" world. But they are rooted in the belief that by observing such inhibitions, a lot of trouble or misunderstanding can be avoided. And that is the point: Avoiding what may become a misunderstanding lest it become a disaster.

Establishing Procedures for Dealing with Misconduct

There is a need for caution (1 Timothy 5:19) when an accusation is made against an elder. Having had some experience of cases of clergy or leader sexual misconduct,I have become clear about a number of general points:

- Church government's immediate reaction is to protect the offender and the church.
- Even when the truth is known, there is a strong initial desire to protect the offender and to mitigate the consequences.
- There is little initial compassion or concern for the victim, who is often seen as a "scarlet woman" taking most of the blame.
- Church government want a clean resolution, usually involving separation of the pastor into some form of rehabilitation and a general "not welcome" sign for the victim.
- Even other clergy may take a very hands-off approach, perhaps recognizing that "there but for the grace of God go I."
- Church government interest in the rehabilitation is short lived, once the problem of separation has been solved.
- Offenders tend to see themselves as victims too, and want to be treated as such. I think this should be resisted as it is essentially manipulative.
- Repentance is often assumed when it may be more properly described as remorse at being caught out. The key to true repentance may lie in the real level of concern expressed by the offender for the victim.

Over several general misconduct cases, I have tried to do what is best for all. I now conclude that trying to put a good face on a bad position is just wrong. However hard one tries to manage the situation, full disclosure will become essential at some point, and attempts to exercise damage control will be fruitless and will be misinterpreted by some in the congregation. Even where full disclosure appears harsh and unloving, it may still be the best course. Offenders will usually use any means to protect their image in the eyes of their friends. You cannot win the support of the congregation and keep the good will of the offender. The offender will see it as "un-Christian" to reveal his offences; but the offence was his and not ours, and we should not be put into the same box.

One leader, despite a written confession, rationalized his position back to where he had absolved himself. His many admirers in the church felt that he was a victim of "church politics" and that he had been unfairly treated. By trying to protect the leader, we put ourselves in a position where we could not defend our actions without breaching confidences and opening newly healed wounds.

I have learned the hard way that it is folly to try to hide things from a church. Information management is always seen as "spin." If trust in one leader is destroyed, trust in all leaders will be affected.

God is Light (1 John 1:5) and any attempt to use darkness for God's purposes will be counterproductive. Secrecy, manipulation, side-deals, manoeuvring— they all smack of worldliness and calculation, and flourish in the shadows and, in my experience, they do not work in the long run. The church needs procedures that are laid down and that take over when an accusation is made, with both the accuser and the accused being treated with respect and kindness. It is hard to do so when one has not done it before or one has no precedent. Legal procedures provide only a limited guide, based as they are on the presumption of innocence.

But while such procedures should be fair, they must also be very firm. Immediate suspension of the suspected offender is mandatory, and the church should be told that an accusation has been made and must be investigated according to established procedures. That the suspected offender will be hurt, guilty or innocent, is unavoidable and that is why the "taboos" must be very strong, to protect against inadvertent misconduct.

The victim needs to be treated carefully and lovingly. Her side of the story needs to be heard and understood by a sympathetic support group, who should be asked to provide counselling and compassion. Abandonment or shunning is not a Christian response, and neither is judgmental disbelief, even if a period of absence from the church body may be appropriate. Jesus' gentle admonition of the woman caught in adultery should be our guide (John 8 3-11).

Church government should keep the congregation informed of developments but avoid satisfying prurience. It has been my experience and observation that church discipline is problematic. When forced to take a position, a church council may make the right decision. But individual members will start to disassociate themselves from the decision, especially when under personal attack for the decision, and may start to blame the leadership for putting them in such a position. Division easily follows.

I believe that if we have to take disciplinary action (1 Timothy 5:20), for example, suspension or expulsion, then we must also reach out to the offender in Christian love, and seek to restore the hurt, if not the position of responsibility (2 Corinthians 2:6-7). Even this can be misinterpreted and rebound, but I still think it is the right and Christian thing to do. Great care must be taken in how such reaching out is handled and room for misinterpretation diminished.

Churches and church-related activities offer many opportunities for people to act in a more impulsive and generous manner than normal. It is terribly easy for this to become the "primrose path" and for the unwary to fall into sin. Predators will naturally be attracted to such situations and must be guarded against. Vulnerable persons need to be aware and beware of putting themselves into any position where they could be abused.

Victorian standards, now widely lampooned, were soundly based on the assumption that if strict standards of conduct were not maintained and protected, with rules and codes of conduct, then the worst could occur or, at the least, be suspected. In an age when one's character and reputation were determined by the absence of dishonourable conduct, real or imagined, everyone was careful to protect the reputation and character of others. In today's world, at least in the West, personal character and reputation have lost their cachet, but the consequences are that we no longer see the dangers of proximity. We think it quaint to impose gender boundaries, but we fail to do so at our peril. We must return to good old-fashioned common sense. If any action or course of conduct can be misinterpreted, it will be, so we must be pro-active and not allow it to start. In the traditional phrase, it is better to be "old-fashioned" than to "fall into sin."

26

A Blessing for Clergy

DAVID MASTERS

In all your work
May you share the fullness
Of God's life.

May your hands,
Blessed with a mandate of healing
Be used to heal
Never to harm.

May your power
Be innocent and gentle
In the spirit of God
Never cunning nor cynical.

May you speak
With humility
To nurture and empower
Never to dominate.

May your presence
Imbued with presence of God
Be a light
To everyone you meet.

27

The Circle of Hope

LUCIANO KOVACS

Violence is a vicious circle, one that subjugates minds and bodies.
Violence is a trap that alienates humanity from the core of existence
Violence scars for life, fills dreams with nightmares and days with ugly shadows.
Violence creeps in under the skin and lingers there gnawing from beneath.
Violence partners with loneliness and shares wounds with its victims.
 We together can be the circle of hope
Breaking the chains, giving birth to joyful whispers
In partnership men and women rejoin on a peacemaking journey
Restoring dignity to the center of life.
The beauty of sexual expression is tainted when used as a tool of oppression.
In solidarity we walk a new way, we embrace the new dawn.

Part Four
Stopping Abuse for Good

28

Identifying Sexual Predators

MARIE M. FORTUNE

One sexual predator in our midst is one too many," said Morris Chapman, president of the Southern Baptist Convention Executive Committee. "Sexual predators must be stopped. They must be on notice that Southern Baptists are not a harvest field for their devious deeds." Good so far. But the Executive Committee has also determined that the denomination will not create a database to identify sexual predators nor establish a national office to respond to complaints. Not so good.

Their reasoning: polity problems. They say local autonomy of their congregations precludes a centralized list or investigative body. The Convention does not have the authority to prohibit known perpetrators from doing ministry. The local church can hire anyone it wants as a pastor. Now I appreciate the value of a congregational polity. My denomination, the United Church of Christ, also uses this way of organizing itself. But I also have spoken with victims and survivors of Southern Baptist pastors who are very frustrated with the unwillingness of their church to take some institutional action to stop clergy offenders. The words are important. The SBC statement is strong. Their website provides some excellent articles on the sexual abuse of children. But words are not enough.

When the study began in 2006, Oklahoma pastor Wade Burleson suggested the database to track ministers who are "credibly accused of, personally confessed to, or legally been convicted of sexual harassment or abuse." The Executive Committee nixed that idea and now urges local churches to use the U.S. Dept. of Justice database of sexual offenders to do their background checks. Here's the problem: this database or any state police database will only include convicted sex offenders. A minister will show up in that database if he has been reported, prosecuted and convicted of a sex offense. The database will not include ministers who may have been fired by a local church. How is a Baptist church to know that their pastoral candidate is in good standing if there is no Baptist database for sexual predators?

Local churches need all the help they can get to deal with a complaint about clergy misconduct, even if it is their decision what to do about it. The national denominational structure can and should make resources available for training and preparation of local church policies. When the Southern Baptist Convention decides to do a mission project, it doesn't worry about local church autonomy. It provides a mechanism for its local churches to participate in mission efforts. Yet when the health and well-being of its members is on the line, it chooses to speak but not to act. It was fourth-century Bishop John Chrysostom who said, "At all times it is works and actions that we need, not a mere show of words. It is easy for anyone to say or promise something, but it is not so easy to act out that word or promise."

This is an issue that independent, non-denominational churches struggle with all the time. They literally have no denominational structure to turn to for support. Their independence means they are isolated and often lack policies when a complaint comes to them. Even if they want to, they often lack the capacity to act to remove an offending pastor. A lawsuit is their only option. Victims have no other recourse. The Roman Catholic Church in the U.S. has put in place a mechanism with standards and policies to address the abuse of children by clergy. Because of its hierarchical polity, it can mandate action by the dioceses and provide resources to assist them. In responding to clergy misconduct, this is an advantage. Still one wonders why it has taken the Catholic Church so long to begin this process.

All of which serves to remind us that polity is not the problem. Regardless of the structure of a religious institution, it has the capacity to act to address clergy misconduct. It is a matter of using the structure and values it has to guide its action. It is a matter of the will to use every institutional resource available to try to ensure that congregations will be safe places for congregants rather than looking for structural excuses why church leaders don't have to act.

29

Supporting Survivors

MARTIN WEBER

The Hope of Survivors

Shame is the reason I'm so proud to be connected with the Hope of Survivors. Perhaps I should explain. More than any organisation I've known in several decades of pastoral ministry, including law enforcement chaplaincy, The Hope of Survivors (THOS) helps victims feeling ashamed from sexual abuse find dignity, confidence, hope and even joy. And so I'm proud to serve on the executive board of THOS. Shame afflicts most of us to some degree. It's part of the human condition. As a chubby child, I was ashamed of my weight. Parents might be ashamed of their teenagers' bad choices. Reformed "party animals" may feel shame for years of carousing. But the human spirit knows no shame to match that of a sexual abuse victim who has been manipulated into feeling guilty for her predator's sins. And those among them most deeply sunken in shame may be victims of clergy sexual abuse.

It's terrible to be raped by a stranger and worse to be assaulted by one's own biological father. In some ways it is most damaging of all to be the sexual victim of one's spiritual leader. Reasonable people are outraged at a sexual predator who drags a jogger off the trail into the bushes. Society springs to the defence of such victims. As for incest, everyone except enabling relatives is furious about paternal predators. But when it comes to clergy sexual abuse, congregational sympathy usually gravitates to a popular, powerful, preacher. Ironically, victims of clergy sexual abuse often must go outside the church to find a sympathetic heart. Tragically, they may lose not only their trusted spiritual leader but also most, if not all, of their faith community—even close friends. This is where THOS has been such a lifesaver for hundreds of lonely victims of clergy sexual abuse who suffer in solitary shame. THOS helps them realise that:

• As with all professionals, a pastor is responsible for not abusing his trust by allowing—and often planning—the sexualisation of what began as normal interaction between himself and a vulnerable parishioner.

• Sexual abuse is not necessarily scary or painful; often unsuspecting victims are drawn into a close friendship with a pastor that unexpectedly becomes romanticised and then sexualised.

• Clergy romance or sex with a parishioner is not an "affair," because it arises from a power imbalance. Physicians, educators and workplace supervisors understand this. Somehow it seems harder for many churches to accept this, perhaps because of the hero status of a star pastor.

• Most pastors are persons of integrity who never would abuse a member. To preserve this propriety, clergy need education and sometimes counselling to manage their own emotions and attractions as they interact with the vulnerable members of their flock.

• Victims of clergy sexual abuse need and deserve advocates in the church to guide them through a resolution process that emphasises healing rather than vindictiveness.

• Those who survive clergy sexual abuse need not bear the burden of proving to anyone—not even themselves or God—that they are perfect and completely innocent about what happened to them. The Bible says all of us are sinners in need of the grace and forgiveness of God.

• It is possible to forgive one's abuser while also establishing boundaries of protection against further abuse by anyone inside or outside the body of Christ.

• Women who have suffered clergy sexual abuse need to find their primary identity in being God's beloved children; this is more than having merely survived something evil done to them.

Clergy Sexual Abuse

To summarise the tragedy of clergy sexual abuse:
• It is normal, for Christian men and women faithful to their spouses, to feel attracted to other people. Unmet emotional needs tend to multiply this chemistry.

• When a pastor finds himself attracted to a parishioner, it is his or her responsibility as a professional caregiver to recognize the danger and use the responsibility of leadership to prevent the relationship from becoming romanticised.

• Some predatory pastors are so corrupt as to be strategically and compulsively abusive, but many fine pastors become sexually abusive simply because they allow their love for God and their spouses to become less important than their ministry to church members.

• Paradoxically, victims of abuse often take much or most of the blame and shame upon themselves after being drawn into inappropriate sexuality.

• The more likeable and admirable a pastor is, the more a victim of his sexual abuse may suffer shame and guilt. This also is true at the opposite extreme: the more deceptive and manipulative a career predator is, the more likely his victim may suffer increased shame and guilt—the most clever abusers manage to download all blame to the victim.

• Adult victims of clergy sexual abuse need not prove to anyone, even to themselves or to God, that they are totally innocent—all human beings are sinners in need of Christ's saving grace.

• Church leaders and other members typically rally around a popular pastor, despite credible evidence that he is guilty of sexual abuse. Often the church would rather blame his victim than lose a beloved spiritual leader.

• In the aftermath of clergy sexual abuse, most efforts to aid recovery are devoted toward the abuser and his spouse rather than to the victim, who often is abandoned or even expelled from the community of believers. In such cases, The Hope of Survivors often becomes the only hope of surviving clergy sexual abuse.

30

Criminalizing Misconduct

Darryl W. Stephens

In 2009, the National Organization for Women (NOW) of the U.S. called for the criminalization of sexual exploitation of women by clergy.[1] NOW urges state legislatures to make it illegal for a pastor to have sex with a congregant, just as a physician, psychiatrist, or licensed counselor may be held criminally liable for "unlawful sexual relations" with those in their care.[2] Should churches join in this effort to criminalize clergy sexual misconduct?

Sexual misconduct is an immoral act, a violation of the sacred trust of ministry. And religious institutions have been notoriously slow to hold their own clergy accountable for sexual misconduct. This commentary argues that churches are in a much better position to respond to sexual misconduct among clergy than the state, even if churches need the pressure of the state to prompt them to action.

Abuse of Power

Sexual misconduct is not an "affair." Rather, it is professional malfeasance in ministry. The clergyperson has a duty to act in the best interests of the parishioner, to maintain professional boundaries, and to refrain from using that relationship to personal advantage. Sex in a pastoral relationship violates the sacred trust of ministry.

The United Methodist Church (UMC) defines sexual abuse in ministry as "a form of sexual misconduct [that] occurs when a person within a ministerial role of leadership … engages in sexual contact or sexualized behavior with a congregant, client, employee, student, staff member, coworker, or volunteer."[3]

The power of the pastoral office creates a context in which meaningful consent by the parishioner is often impossible. The concept of "meaningful consent" is based on the ability of each party to say "no" without fear of reprisal. Consent is maximized in a relationship of equals. The ability of the more vulnerable party in a relationship to consent to sexual activity is diminished as the power differential increases. In a fiduciary relationship, the professional is trusted not to exploit the imbalance in power to his/her own advantage. Because of the authority of the clergyperson, the disparate power between pastor and parishioner, and the emotional vulnerability of the parishioner, sexual contact within a ministerial relationship lacks true consent even if the parishioner agrees to it. There is no meaningful consent possible in such a relationship because of the disparity of power between the minister and person seeking care.[4]

Confession of Sin

Historically, faith communities have been slow to respond to abuses by clergy. Even as recently as twenty years ago, predatory clergy routinely were given "geographic therapy" by being reappointed somewhere else in the hope that their misconduct would be kept quiet.

It has only been within the past fifteen years that the UMC has explicitly addressed clergy sexual misconduct. General Conference, this denomination's highest policy-making body, passed its first resolution addressing sexual abuse within pastoral relationships in 1996. The same year, "sexual misconduct" entered the UMC lexicon of chargeable clergy offenses.

Sexual misconduct remains a problem, nonetheless. Three percent of women attending church in the past month reported being sexually harassed or abused by a clergyperson at some point in their adult lives, according to a nationwide study in the U.S.[5] Ongoing news reports about clergy sexual misconduct should provide a sobering reminder to every church to confront its own abuse crisis before it blows up as a scandal in national headlines.

We must confess our collective sin: "We have failed to be an obedient church…and we have not heard the cry of the needy." In secular language, NOW President Terry O'Neill explains: "Law enforcement authorities need to step up their investigations of sexual abuse in religious organizations because it is apparent that many church officials will not act in a prompt and responsible manner."

The State[6]

NOW's resolution would add clergy to existing state laws covering other counseling relationships. Nearly every state in the United States criminalizes sexual contact between secular counselors or "mental health professionals" and their clients. Only thirteen states include clergy in these laws, which are based on legal concepts of fiduciary duty and professional standard of care. Only two states criminalize sexual contact between clergy and congregant outside of a formal counseling relationship.

From a legal standpoint, though, NOW's approach may not be as effective as taking a different tack to avoid unnecessary entanglements between church and state in U.S. constitutional law. A statutory focus on lack of meaningful consent rather than fiduciary duty may provide the legal traction necessary for states to criminalize clergy misconduct.

Courts are hesitant to intervene in cases involving adult-to-adult relationships in religious institutions. The U.S. criminal justice system is constitutionally limited in its ability to address clergy misconduct due to separation of church and state. As a consequence, secular courts cannot rule on the standard of care appropriate to a pastoral counseling relationship. Clergy cannot be convicted of malpractice because the state cannot legally define the "practice" of a religious professional.

Identifying the lack of consent within a relationship based on power and authority is within the court's purview, though. As with laws protecting minors, the mentally impaired, intoxicated persons or others whose consent might be easily coerced, this approach would protect the vulnerable party and does not ask courts to rule on religious questions.

The Church

While state laws may provide some degree of public accountability for clergy, the church is much better situated than the state to protect the integrity of the ministerial relationship. Churches can clearly communicate appropriate interpersonal boundaries, the differential in power inherent in a pastoral relationship, and the fiduciary duty of the minister. Churches must also hold all persons in a ministerial role of leadership accountable to these standards. Lack of clarity about the nature of the pastoral relationship and lack of moral will to address the problem of clergy misconduct are at the root of the church's failure to provide justice for the vulnerable.

Criminal statutes would help bring accountability to churches. For example, churches in the U.S. did not begin to address sexual harassment until the 1980s, prompted by the Equal Employment Opportunity Commission (EEOC) and a U.S. Supreme Court case upholding EEOC guidelines and reporting mechanisms. Only then did the UMC make its first official stand against the sin of sexual harassment in 1988.

From a practical standpoint, criminalizing clergy misconduct may also provide external support to churches seeking to investigate allegations of misconduct. Judicatory leaders would be able to rely on the trained expertise of law enforcement officers to conduct investigations and handle evidence (such as DNA samples), in the same that way child abuse cases are handled now. The state would also maintain clear jurisdiction even when a clergyperson surrenders ministerial credentials. The church often has difficulty bringing an investigation to conclusion if an accused clergyperson leaves the ministry prior to adjudication. Justice is derailed for all parties when there is no determination of guilt or innocence.

The church cannot delegate responsibility to the state for determining ethical standards for clergy, but where a clear professional relationship exists that restricts freedom of consent, abuse of pastoral power should be against the law. Criminalization of clergy misconduct may have the positive effect of deterring would-be clergy sexual predators, protecting potential victims and promoting clarity about sexual activity in ministry as an abuse of power. State intervention would call the church to accountability.

31

Fundamental Reform

TERRY O'NEILL

Law enforcement authorities need to step up their investigations of sexual abuse in religious organizations because it is apparent that many church officials will not act in a prompt and responsible manner," National Organization for Women President Terry O'Neill stated. "In addition, state laws must clearly define the role of a priest or pastor as one involving a 'fiduciary duty' between a licensed caregiver and a client—like those accorded psychiatrists or physicians. Sexual relations in those instances should be grounds for appropriate civil as well as criminal sanctions."

Recent reports from European and other countries about physical and sexual abuse of children by Catholic priests and cover-up by those in authority demand swift and effective action. The emerging facts about the church's behind-the-scenes actions are appalling: allowing the sexual exploitation of girls and women, including nuns; procuring abortions for those who became pregnant and intimidating them into silence; and using church officials to "wipe down the crime scene."

"When an all-male church hierarchy poses as unquestioned authority, the potential for abuse and cover-up is great," O'Neill said. "Religious organizations without a strong laity or democratic governance have failed to take the necessary steps. Church members, abuse survivors and their advocates must demand accountability."

"In addition to stepped-up legal recourse, fundamental reform of the male-dominated Catholic Church is needed if children and women are to be protected from predatory priests—and if the church is to regain some modicum of moral authority," O'Neill said. "The best reform would begin with bringing women into positions of power. Until that happens, with its current track record of sexual exploitation, the church is in no position to make pronouncements on the roles or rights of women."

NOW's membership is speaking out against clergy sexual abuse. Not only are children—girls as much as boys—the victims of sexual exploitation, but adult women also are at risk. Reports of the latter cases are slow to surface, perhaps because of the shame felt by the victims and efforts by church leaders to keep reports from becoming public. A number of studies in the United States show that adult women are even more likely than children to be targets of clergy who use their positions of trust for sexual exploitation. A Ford Foundation-Baylor University survey in 2008 found that one in 33 women had experienced sexual abuse by their priest or pastor. These are not "relationships" but rather the abusive exercise of power. The outcomes can be devastating. Clinical reports indicate high rates of post-traumatic stress disorder, other anxiety disorders, depression, physical illness and suicide, according to the FaithTrust Institute.[1]

National Organization for Women

Call to Criminalize Sexual Exploitation of Women by Clergy

WHEREAS, the National Organization for Women (NOW) has fought hard to shatter societal silence regarding all forms of sexual violence; and

WHEREAS, public misunderstanding and lack of knowledge regarding adult victims of sexual exploitation by clergy have contributed to silencing the voices of these victims; and

WHEREAS, the overwhelming majority of victims of sexual exploitation by clergy are adults, predominately female congregants victimized by male clergy; and

WHEREAS, adult victims of clergy sexual exploitation are routinely blamed for this abuse and revictimized by the public, severely ostracized by their own congregations, and disbelieved by religious authority figures from whom they seek solace and protection, resulting in devastating social isolation and confusion; and

WHEREAS, in addition to coping with the physical and emotional impacts of sexual violation, victims of sexual exploitation by clergy often also suffer loss of faith, loss of religious tradition, loss of spouse, loss of employment within religious organizations or with faith-affiliated educational institutions, self-blame by the victim, and loss of support from family, congregation, and community;

THEREFORE BE IT RESOLVED, that NOW chapters be encouraged to participate in educational and advocacy campaigns to increase public awareness that the majority of victims of clergy sexual exploitation are adult women and that sexual violation by a spiritual leader has profound life-altering impacts; and

BE IT FURTHER RESOLVED, that NOW entities be encouraged to support state legislative campaigns for statutory reform, in particular to add clergy to the enumerated categories of professionals covered in fiduciary-duty laws in states having such laws, and for criminalization of sexual relations between similarly enumerated categories of professionals in states not having fiduciary-duty laws; and

BE IT FINALLY RESOLVED, that NOW disseminate information on the extent and impacts of clergy sexual exploitation of adult women, including legal avenues of redress and model legislation, on the NOW website and via other media outlets that NOW regularly utilizes for its advocacy campaigns.

32

Dragging Sextortion into the Light

CLÉO FATOOREHCHI

In their 2010 book *Half the Sky,* Pulitzer Prize-winners Nicholas Kristof and Sheryl WuDunn write about a disturbing but not uncommon problem in Southern Africa—male teachers who trade good grades for sex with students. The authors note that "half of Tanzanian women, and nearly half of Ugandan women, say they were abused by male teachers."

What Is Sextortion?

There's a word for this—*sextortion.* The main characteristic of sextortion cases is that they involve a perpetrator in a position of influence or authority, Joan Winship, executive director of the International Association of Women Judges (IAWJ), told the United Nations Inter Press Service (IPS). This includes teachers but also policemen, priests or employers, for example. "There is (also) an element of *quid pro quo,* where, if you agree to have sex, then I will be able to give you a promotion, or a raise, or your visa, or I will not give you a traffic ticket. So there is an element of exchange there, which can be either explicit or implicit," she explained.

These elements of exchange and power imply consent from the victim, and "that makes it a challenge (to prosecute)," said Winship. "It's part of the problem why it hasn't been defined, and this is what we're trying to do." The IAWJ used a recent meeting of the Commission on the Status of Women in New York as an opportunity to shed light on sextortion.

Ending Impunity

Sextortion is a widespread phenomenon, found in all countries of the world. But since it is mostly unreported, impunity is common for perpetrators. It is with the goal of ending this impunity that IAWJ launched a programme entitled "Stopping the Abuse of Power for Purposes of Sexual Exploitation: Naming,

157

Shaming, and Ending Sextortion" in March 2009 in The Hague. Aided by the government of the Netherlands through its MDG3 Fund, the programme pulls together three of IAWJ's partners, from Tanzania, the Philippines, and Bosnia-Herzegovina. The concrete outcome of this initiative is the creation of a toolkit that will provide judges with a range of current laws that can be applied to cases of sextortion (see www.IAWJ.org). As Hon. Teresita de Castro, from the Supreme Court of the Philippines, highlighted during a panel on the issue, when people understand that sextortion is a crime, then justice can be done.

Victims of sextortion also need to see it as a crime and overcome their fear of speaking out, even though "when they do come forward, there are other obstacles [for prosecution]," said Nancy Hendry, IAWJ senior legal advisor. "She or he stands alone, not only against the individual defendant, but also against the entire institution that the defendant represents—and historically, the community that has invested its trust in the defendant," Anne Goldstein, IAWJ human rights education director, told IPS.

IAWJ is not advocating for a new legal framework on this issue, either at the country or international level. "The problem is not an absence of law, the problem is the absence of will to enforce [existing] laws," Goldstein said.

IAWJ considers sextortion "a form of corruption," in which it is not money but sex that is at stake. But while reparations can be made for financial corruption, sextortion brings psychological and physical damage, and overall is much more dangerous, Justice de Castro underlined.

IAWJ is lobbying to have existing anti-corruption laws used to prosecute sextortion perpetrators. Goldstein told IPS their purpose is to "draw together in one place both the anti-Gender Based Violence laws and the anti-corruption laws that are generally looked at separately but—IAWJ believes—need to be integrated." "A successful strategy against sextortion would mainstream anti-corruption efforts into gender—and vice versa," she said. As Winship concludes, "We want to change the thinking that the currency does not have to be only money; the currency can be asking for sex."

Using the Internet to Fight Back

The internet is usually viewed as increasing the potential for various forms of sexual abuse, such as by the hacking of webcams or computers in search of compromising photos. Teenagers are the most affected by this new trend, since they are easily intimidated.

However, IAWJ considers the internet a useful tool "for victims [of sextortion] to find each other, share stories and offer support," Goldstein told IPS. "Thus, you have groups springing up such as SNAP (the Survivors Network of those Abused by Priests) and STAMP (Survivors Take Action against Military Personnel)."

She also pointed out that if "it's easy to brush aside a single allegation of sexual abuse/sexual harassment/sextortion, it's much harder to ignore thousands." She cited the examples of the 2004 John Jay College of Criminal Justice report, "The Nature and Scope of the Problem of Sexual Abuse of Minors by Catholic Priests and Deacons in the United States," which "brought together 10,667 complaints against 4,392 individual priests." In addition, "sexual harassment—the *quid pro quo* form of which is a canonical example of sextortion—went from being something that "just happened" to women, to "a violation of the law."

Finally, new technologies represent a tremendous tool for providing allegations of sexual extortion. "It is no coincidence that many of the sextortion cases that have led to actual court convictions involved compromising e-mails, texts, audio or video recordings," said Goldstein.

Thanks to these new tools, concluded Goldstein, "at least we have been able to move from denial or blaming a few rotten apples to the acknowledgment that sexual abuse/harassment/sextortion are serious problems embedded in institutional cultures—and they need to be addressed."

33

Protecting the Vulnerable

M. Garlinda Burton

Once again, the Roman Catholic Church is in the hot seat in the wake of allegations of sexual misconduct by priests and cover-ups at the highest levels of church leadership. And once again, the leadership has flubbed it—blaming news media, playing the victim, making excuses and generally not taking responsibility. The pope, arguably the world's most prolific theologian, can't even offer a simple apology.

However, lest the rest of us in the religious community yield to the temptation to sit in smug and detached judgment of our brothers in the Catholic hierarchy, let's consider the planks in our own eyes.

Church Mutual Insurance, a company that insures churches and church-related entities from several denominations, reportedly receives more than 350 claims per year regarding alleged sexual abuse of adults and children by clergy or laity in ministerial leadership.

In the United Methodist Church, adjudicating cases of sexual misconduct by clergy has cost us $100 million in the past 10 years alone. (And those are just the cases we know about. There is no central repository for such records. So, if you don't have enough money to pay your pastor's salary, give scholarships to all your college-age members, or send a mission team to build a well in Haiti, this is one reason why.)

Beyond that, so far in 2010, the churchwide Commission on the Status and Role of Women has fielded 40 complaints of alleged sexual abuse against women, children and men by United Methodist clergy and laity in ministerial and church leadership roles.

The United Methodist Church has a commendable track record in terms of on-the-books policies and procedures for screening clergy candidates, prevention training for active pastors, adjudication of complaints and cooperating with civil authorities. However, our actual track record for effective prevention, intervention and holding errant clergy accountable for abuse is another thing. As in

160

the Roman Catholic situation, too often we protect bad pastors by simply moving them to new assignments, we don't communicate well with affected congregations and we neglect and marginalize those who are abused—sometimes even ostracizing and punishing "whistle blowers" for reporting misconduct.

In fact, too often, the corporate United Methodist Church neglects our primary call to be caring and pastoral to wounded disciples of Jesus Christ in the name of protecting the institutional church, discrediting those who complain and engaging in stonewalling and legal maneuvering instead of justice making.

And each time we fail to protect the vulnerable we sacrifice a bit more of our integrity, credibility and ability to reflect and represent the loving and liberating gospel of Jesus Christ.

I've been asked by journalists and church leaders alike: "What do you think about the Catholic situation?" and "What advice would you give to Catholic church leaders?" And my answer, humbly, is, that every Christian community— its leaders and everyday members alike—must take the following steps to reclaim moral authority, using this to-do list.

• *Confront sexism, ageism and racism.* Most perpetrators of sexual abuse are men; most of the abused are women and children. One reason Christians can't get a handle on abuse is because we privilege males—particularly clergy males—and we discount and dismiss women and children. We as a society believe that women are intentionally provocative and are "asking for it." We believe that children lie and that teenage girls asserting their sexual beings can seduce and lead a grown man astray. Too often, we people of color and those from the Southern Hemisphere defend sexism and sexual violence as "cultural norms" and, therefore, acceptable. However, in claiming the Gospel of Jesus Christ as our road map for individual and corporate life, we also declare that the sacred worth of all people trumps sexism, ageism and culture. We need to say that and live it.

• *Remove errant pastors.* Period. Being ordained or licensed as a minister is not a right—it is a calling and a privilege. Ordination is the church's imprimatur on our representatives, who are not perfect, but who are called and set apart by God as servant leaders. Clergy (and laypersons serving ministerial roles)—who use their parishes as their harems, who exploit children and vulnerable adults and who operate out of a sense of maverick entitlement harm the church and its members. They are not effective ministers of grace, they cannot be trusted to represent the Gospel of Jesus Christ in a hurting world, and they have no place teaching and preaching in the name of our church. Errant clergy are, of course, recipients of God's love, redemption and forgiveness. Removing pastors who exhibit bad behavior and offering them redeeming love and pastoral support are not mutually exclusive.

• *Support and reward good pastors.* Being an effective, caring, healthy pastor is a hard job, and a disproportionate number of pastors neglect their personal lives and let boundaries between church and home slide. When this happens, even good pastors are at risk of losing their perspective, crossing personal boundaries, and messing up. Clergy need regularly scheduled renewal leave and pastoral care outside their official assignments. Pastors need days off; married pastors need date nights; single pastors need time and space to date and socialize. In a recent conversation, a pastor-friend told me she has so much paperwork, so many meetings and so much day-to-day work that she seldom has time for group Bible study and intense prayer, and that her district superintendent has never asked her, "How is it with your soul?" Nurturing and sustaining effective pastors requires us to tend to their souls, to make discipleship development an ongoing part of our support and continuing education, and to have systems in place to intervene when a clergyperson is in trouble. The first step in preventing sexual misconduct by clergy is to ensure that the pastors we claim—beginning in seminary and in the local-pastor licensing processes—are supported and affirmed for their ongoing spiritual and emotional well-being.

• *Engage laypeople in prevention.* Most laypeople depend on pastors and church administrators to set the standards, know the rules about professional boundaries and abuse-of-power issues, maintain the appropriate boundaries and hold clergy accountable. However, I believe educating laity and letting laity take part in both prevention education and adjudication would help prevent secret keeping and the temptation for clergy to shield errant colleagues. Laity need to know that misconduct does happen in the church and that we have policies and procedures for addressing it, and that their protection and their spiritual and physical well-being are uppermost in the minds of pastors, bishops and other church leaders. Back-room deals, hiding behind "confidentiality" agreements, and moving bad pastors to other appointments has not stemmed the number of sexual abuse cases. There are laity in the pews who are psychiatrists, therapists, educators, lawyers and teachers; they've dealt with professional boundary issues for decades and can only help the church get its house in order.

• *Uphold nonnegotiable, binding churchwide policies, procedures and adjudication.* Currently, except for minimum standards, each annual conference of The United Methodist Church sets its own standards for ordaining/licensing ministers. Each conference designs its own method and manner for training and orienting pastors and church members, and each conference has its own processes and standards for dealing with sexual misconduct (and any other complaints), including caring for the accuser, accused, their families and congregations. These standards, practices and processes can vary widely according to the competency of bishops and other administrators and their interest and sensitivity. They may also vary by geographical location and cultural history. That's not good enough. If we are The United Methodist Church of Jesus Christ, seeking to transform the world in his name, then we need to assure that wherever the Cross and Flame is found, that clergy and laity in leadership are bound by equally high standards and will be held accountable if they cross certain strict boundaries, i.e., perpetrating sexual abuse or misconduct.

• *Confess our sins publicly and then make it right.* As anyone who has ever fought with a spouse knows, saying, "I'm sorry you feel hurt" is worse than saying nothing at all. Still worse is playing the victim, as some Catholic leaders have done when they claim that the media is picking on the church by reporting on the sexual abuse scandal. Reality check: "The only victims are the ones who were abused by the church and saw their abusers go unpunished." The only godly stance when a Christian has wronged another, who is made in God's image, is to humbly admit wrongdoing (publicly and often), to beg forgiveness from and offer restitution to God and the survivors, to seek justice for those affected, and to work tirelessly to ensure that the wrongdoing is not repeated.

Yes, the current news is full of the "Catholic problem," but be assured that clergy sexual misconduct is an ecumenical problem that requires all Christians be equipped to know the issues, act appropriately, pray for forgiveness and wisdom, and to humbly pledge that we will cease making protections for errant clergy and negligent denominational leaders a higher priority than serving and protecting the people God has placed in our care.

34

A Safe Place

GARY R. SCHOENER

The church, even for non-believers, is a *sanctuary—a safe place.* Beyond a place to worship, a church is a place where one may bring one's concerns and problems. While the Nathan Network has been focused on dealing with sexual abuse in the church—a way in which the church is not a safe place— parishioners and others may bring to the church a number of problems from the outside world:

(1) Family violence—abuse by spouse who may, or may not be a church member

(2) Family violence caused by abusive kids who may be engaging in drug use and criminal activity

(3) Being a victim of physical or sexual violence in the community

(4) Being a victim of economic crime, such as fraud

(5) Serious economic hardships

(6) Bullying and sexual harassment in the workplace

(7) Sexual exploitation outside the church.

Besides sexual harassment or sexual exploitation by ordained persons–a pastor or deacon–these same things may be the result of actions by other church staff or church members. In addition, there are also non-sexual offenses, such as someone who is excessively manipulative or who engages in "power plays" or someone who is abusive or harassing. Within each area, the questions are: What role does the church want to play? What is involved in taking on this role? What tools does the church have to resolve such problems?

Our Experience and Knowledge

How far have we come in dealing with the abuse of women in the church?

Response and Resolution. There are many models for response and resolution, depending on how organized the church is and the situation. If the offense is admitted, one can focus on remedy. If it is denied, there may be a battle over the truth. In this case, it is more difficult to reach a solution.

Processing and Mediation. These are two ways of resolving disputes and problems, but both have limitations. One of the big challenges is that people have very different views of what is an acceptable outcome. We should be clear about our goals and clear about confidentiality.

Accountability. Beware of quick admissions of guilt and confessions. Is there really remorse? Is there accountability for the outcome? Rev. Marie Fortune and others feel that restitution is a key component. There is disagreement as to whether this must come from the offender, from the church or from the church's insurance company. Be aware that there is a tendency to jump to conclusions before an investigation is undertaken.

Truth Telling. This has to do with communicating with the congregation. The particular congregation and parties involved have a major influence on how truth is discovered or revealed.

(1) Be very careful about asking the involved parties how the situation should be revealed; do not promise to do it their way.

(2) Do not assume that the Parish Council or church leaders will maintain confidentiality.

(3) Do not delay too long because the rumors (started with by the offender or victim) will travel quickly

(4) What is written may find its way around the community.

(5) Having people (pastor or victim) tell their version sometimes helps clear the air but it may so be used for manipulation.

Assisting Victims. Because most communities do not have support groups, much of the counseling will be individual.. There is a clear role of the church to pay for services. Some internet options are helpful (FORUM, HOPETALK, ADVOCATEWEB).

Evaluating the Offender. There is no one accepted approach or protocol. There is the problem of evaluating rehabilitation.

Stages in Handling the Crisis

Pre-Crisis. Sometimes persons know about the situation and either don't act or act in a fashion which is ineffective. *We struggle with truth while we want to avoid suspicion and reporting on each other.*

Crisis. There is no formula for what to do when a story breaks or a complaint is received. Confidentiality makes a difference. Keep in mind that emotions and confusion are central and that the key need is to begin the investigation while providing information as needed and assuring people that you will get to the bottom of it.

Processing. After the crisis has broken, the congregation and leadership begin trying to deal with the situation:

(1) Victim-blaming is common.

(2) Polarization occurs with those divided by those who support and those who condemn the offender

(3) There may be considerable fear for the future of the church.

Resolution. The crisis will end and solutions will be found. The final version of the story will be disseminated. Some leave, some stay with the church. Decisions will be made on the fate of the pastor and the fate of the victim.

There will be sometimes a second group of those who have been the victims of exploitation, who feel that the church has not done enough for reconciliation. They appeal to people for a mediation or reconciliation. It is unclear whether anything would actually bring that about, because the more they make a point of their alienation, the more others exclude them, which creates more alienation, and so on.

Some Questions

Many further questions naturally arise:

(1) How far should the church go in addressing social problems which affect both individuals and families?

(2) What has priority?

(3) How does one balance ministries that help individuals and families?. They compete for time and resources.

(4) Are support groups a resource?'

(5) Are partnerships with other organizations and groups an option?

(6) With declining resources, the church is challenged monetarily in *how much the church can do.*

(7) The church's own house has to be "clean." Attempts must be made to remove power politics and social games as much as possible.

Related Issues

Joint ventures and social programming out of churches might be a useful way to address broader societal issues. Interfaith task forces or consultative groups have great value in terms of consultation regarding troublesome cases. The Mennonite Reconciliation Service and Women's Committee are examples of mediation.

There are in Minnesota (and elsewhere) joint ventures among churches for social projects. A number of churches put together a Neighborhood Involvement Program which has many services. They also collaborate on housing. One local social justice foundation sponsors a walk involving many of non-profits, including my own (www.walkforjustice.kintera.org). Another group sponsored guest lectures.

Last but not least, when the church gets involved there is always liability, not just legal liability but challenges if efforts fall short in someone's eyes.

Notes

1. Historical Reflections of Clergy Sexual Abuse • *Gary R. Schoener*

1. Lloyd, G.E.R., ed. (1983). *Hippocratic Writings*. London: Penguin Classics.

2. Ibid.

3. Braceland, F. (1969). "Historical Perspectives of the Ethical Practice of Psychiatry." *American Journal of Psychiatry* 126, pp. 230-37; 236.

4. Stark, 1989, p. 793.

5. Sipe, *A Secret World*. Routledge, 1990.

6. Franklin, de Bory, Lavoisier, Bailly, Majault, Sallin, d'Arcet, Guillotin, and Le Roy, 1965, p. 6.

7. Perry (1979), 188. Cited in Russell G. Smith, ed., *Health Care, Crime, and Regulatory Control*. Annondale, NSW, Aus.: Hawkins, n.d.

8. Gedge, Karin E. (2003). *Without Benefit of Clergy: Women and the Pastoral Relationship in Nineteenth-Century American Culture*. New York, NY: Oxford University Press. Karin Gege is an assistant history professor at West Chester University in Pennsylvania. The *Onderdonk* case below is from *Without Benefit of Clergy*.

9. Schoener, Gary; Milgrom, Jeanette; Gonsiorek, John; Luepker, Ellen; and Conroe, Ray. (1989*). Psychotherapists' Sexual Involvement With Clients: Intervention and Prevention*. Minneapolis, Minnesota: Walk-In Counseling Center, 837.

10. Ibid., 837.

11. Reid, Darnel; Linder, Robert; Shelly, Bruce; and Stout, Harry. (Eds.). (1990) *Dictionary of Christianity in America*. Downers Grove, Illinois: Intervarsity Press.

12. Morey, Ann-Janine. (Oct. 5, 1988). "Blaming Women for the SexuallyActive Male Pastor." *The Christian Century*, pp.866-69.

13. Ibid, 868,

14. Gabriel, Mary (1998). *Notorious Victoria: The Life of Victoria Woodhull, Uncensored*. Chapel Hill, N.C.: Algonquin Books of Chapel Hill.

15. Waller, Altina. (1982). *Reverend Beecher and Mrs. Tilton*. Boston, Mass.: University of Mass. Press.

16. Hawthorne, Nathaniel. (1991). *The Scarlet Letter*. Philadelphia, Penna.: Courage Books. (Originally published in 1850 by Ticknor, Reed, and Fields.), 134.

17. Morey, Ann-Janine, "Blaming Women for the SexuallyActive Male Pastor."

18 Harris, Corra. (1988). *The Circuit Rider's Wife*. Wilmore, Kentucky: Bristol Books. (Originally published in 1910), 81-83.

19. Ibid., 83-84.

20. Ibid., 85.

21. Turnbull, Agnes. (1948*). The Bishop's Mantle*. New York: Macmillan Co., 235. *Emphasis mine.*

22. Ed. James Strachey. New York: Norton, 1990.

23. Carotenuto, Aldo. (1984). A Secret Symmetry: Sabina Spielrein between Jung and Freud. New York: Pantheon Books.

24. McGuire, William (ed.). (1988). *The Freud/Jung Letters: The Correspondence between Sigmund Freud and C.G. Jung*. Cambridge, Mass.: Harvard University Press. 228.

25. Ibid, 230.

26. Ibid., 231.

27. Ibid., 236.

28. Donn, Linda. (1990). *Freud and Jung: Years of Friendship, Years of Loss*. New York: Collier Books, 93.

29. McGuire, 1988, p. 8.

30. New York: Vintage, 1994, 379.

31. Schoener et. al., 1989, pp. 25-45.

32. Lucy Freeman and Julie Roy, *Betrayal*. Book World, 1976 [1900].

33. Holroyd, Jean, and Brodsky, Annette. (1977). "Psychologists' Attitudes and Pratices regarding Erotic and Nonerotic Physical Contact with Patients." *American Psychologist*, 32, pp. 843-49.

34. Bisbing, Steve, Jorgenson, Linda; and Sutherland, Pamela (1996*). Sexual Abuse by Professionals: A Legal Guide*. Charlottesville, Va.: Michie, 1995.

35. The program can be found in Schoener et. al., 1989, pp. 787-92.

36. Thousand Oaks, Calif.: Sage, 1995.

37. Schoener et. al., 1989, pp. 203-13.

38. Ibid., 177-202.

Works Cited in Chapter 1

Bisbing, Steve; Jorgenson, Linda; and Sutherland, Pamela (1996). *Sexual Abuse by Professionals: A Legal Guide.* Charlottesville, Virginia: Michie Company.

Bouhoutsos, J.; Holroyd, J.; Lerman, H.; Forer, B.; and Greenberg, M. (1983). *Sexual Intimacy between Psychotherapists and Patients.* Professional Psychology: Research and Practice, 14, pp. 185-96.

Braceland, F. (1969). "Historical Perspectives of the Ethical Practice of Psychiatry." *American Journal of Psychiatry*, 126, pp. 230-37.

Burgess, Ann and Hartman, Carol.(Eds.) (1986). *Sexual Exploitation of Patients by Health Professionals.* New York: Praeger.

Carotenuto, Aldo. (1984). *A Secret Symmetry: Sabina Spielrein Between Jung and Freud.* New York: Pantheon Books.

Chesler, Phyllis. (1972). *Women and Madness.* New York: Avon Books.

Donn, Linda. (1990). *Freud and Jung: Years of Friendship, Years of Loss.* New York: Collier Books.

Fitzgerald, F. Scott. (1933). *Tender Is the Night.* New York: Charles Scribner's.

Fortune, Marie. (1989). *Is Nothing Sacred?* New York: Harper and Row.

Gabriel, Mary (1998). *Notorious Victoria: The Life of Victoria Woodhull, Uncensored.* Chapel Hill, N.C.: Algonquin Books of Chapel Hill.

Gardner, Helen. (Ed.).(1987). *The New Oxford Book of English Verse* 1250-1950. Oxford: Oxford University Press.

Gedge, Karin E. (2003). *Without Benefit of Clergy: Women and the Pastoral Relationship in Nineteenth-Century American Culture.* New York, NY: Oxford University Press.

Harris, Corra. (1988). *The Circuit Rider's Wife.* Wilmore, Kentucky: Bristol Books. (Originally published in 1910.).

Hawthorne, Nathaniel. (1991). *The Scarlet Letter.* Philadelphia, Penna.: Courage Books. (Originally published in 1850 by Ticknor, Reed, and Fields.)

Holroyd, Jean and Brodsky, Annette. (1977). "Psychologists' Attitudes and Pratices regarding Erotic and Nonerotic Physical Contact with Patients." *American Psychologist*, 32, pp. 843-49.

Jones, Ernest. (1953). *The Life and Work of Sigmund Freud*, Vol. 1. New York: Basic.

Lloyd, G.E.R. (Ed.). (1983). *Hippocratic Writings.* London: Penguin Classics.

Masters, William and Johnson, Virginia. (1970). *Human Sexual Inadequacy.* Boston, Mass.: Little, Brown and Co.

Masters, William and Johnson, Virginia. (1975). "Principles of the New Sex Therapy." Paper delivered at the annual meeting of the American Psychiatric Association, Anaheim, California.

McCartney, J.L. (1966). "Overt Transference." *Journal of Sex Research*, 2, pp. 227-37.

McGuire, William. (Ed.). (1988). *The Freud/Jung Letters: The Correspondence Between Sigmund Freud and C.G. Jung*. Cambridge, Mass.: Harvard University Press.

Minnesota Interfaith Committee on Sexual Exploitation by Clergy (1989). Sexual Exploitation by Clergy: Reflections and Guidelines for Religious Leaders. Minneapolis, Minnesota: Author.

Morey, Ann-Janine. (Oct. 5, 1988). "Blaming Women for the Sexually ve Male Pastor." The Christian Century, pp.866-69.

Reid, Darnel; Linder, Robert; Shelly, Bruce; and Stout, Harry. (Eds.). (1990) *Dictionary of Christianity in America*. Downers Grove, Illinois: Intervarsity Press.

Reiser, S.J.; Dyck, A.J.; and Curran, W.J. (1977). *Ethics in Medicine--Historical Perspectives and Contemporary Concerns*. Cambridge, Mass.: MIT Press.

Rutter, Peter. (1989*). Sex in the Forbidden Zone: When Therapists, Doctors, Clergy, Teachers and Other Men in Power betray Women's Trust*. Los Angeles, Calif.: Jeremy P. Tarcher.

Schoener, Gary; Milgrom, Jeanette; Gonsiorek, John; Luepker, Ellen; and Conroe, Ray. (1989*). Psychotherapists' Sexual Involvement With Clients: Intervention and Prevention*. Minneapolis, Minnesota: Walk-In Counseling Center.

Turnbull, Agnes. (1948*). The Bishop's Mantle*. New York: Macmillan Co.

Waller, Altina. (1982). *Reverend Beecher and Mrs. Tilton*. Boston, Mass.: University of Mass. Press.

Washington Council of Churches. (1984*). Sexual Contact by Pastors and Pastoral Counselors in Professional Relationships*. Seattle, Washington. D.C.

Weber, M. (Jan. 1972). "Should You Sleep with Your Therapist? The Raging Controversy in American Psychiatry." *Vogue*, pp. 78-9.

2. Sexual Abuse by Religious Leaders • Marie M. Fortune

1. It is not unusual for people who are exploited by a religious leader or pastoral counselor to have some history of childhood sexual abuse, or abuse within an adult intimate relationship, which may not have been addressed. Disclosing child sexual abuse or current domestic violence only increases their vulnerability to further exploitation by a religious leader.

2. For Jews and Christians, the mandate to protect the vulnerable derives from the Hebrew hospitality code.

3. Clergy Sexual Misconduct • Diane R. Garland

1. The coinvestigators of this study are Diana R. Garland, LCSW, Ph.D., Dean and Professor of Social Work, Baylor University; and Mark Chaves, Ph.D., Professor of Sociology, Religion, and Divinity, Duke University. The study is reported in two forthcoming articles. *Journal of the Scientific Study of Religion* will publish Chaves and Garland, "The Prevalence of Clergy Sexual Advances towards Adults in their Congregations"; and the journal *Social Work and Christianity* will publish Garland and Argueta, "How Clergy Sexual Misconduct Happens: A Qualitative Study of First-Hand Accounts."

5. Systemic Collusion • Dee Ann Miller

1. See www.takecourage.org/defining.

2. See www.takecourage.org/treatment.

3. For more insights, see *Striking Parallels and Contrasts,* at takecourage.org/parallels.

6. The Sacred Trust of Ministry • Darryl W. Stephens

1. For a helpful explanation of the concept of justice in the Bible, see Nicholas Wolterstorff, "Justice, Not Charity: Social Work through the Eyes of Faith," *Social Work and Christianity* 33, no. 2 (2006).

2. *The United Methodist Hymnal* (Nashville: UM Publishing House, 1989), 35.

3. "Sexual Misconduct within Ministerial Relationships," *The Book of Resolutions of The United Methodist Church 2008* (Nashville: UM Publishing House, 2008), 134-5.

4. For an excellent discussion on power and vulnerability in ministry, see Marie M. Fortune, *Responding to Clergy Misconduct: A Handbook* (Seattle: FaithTrust Institute, 2009), 41-5.

5. Marie M. Fortune, *Love Does No Harm: Sexual Ethics for the Rest of Us* (New York: Continuum, 1995), 42.

6. For a similar treatment of the ambiguities of the moral terrain of ministry, from an evangelical Christian Realist perspective, see Rebekah Miles, *The Pastor as Moral Guide* (Minneapolis: Fortress Press, 1999).

7. The concept of "meaningful consent" is based on the ability of each party to say "no," without fear of reprisal. Consent is maximized in a relationship of equals. The ability of the more vulnerable party in a relationship to consent to sexual activity is diminished as the power differential increases. In a fiduciary relationship, the professional is trusted not to exploit the imbalance in power to his/her own advantage. On the lack of meaningful consent to sexual intimacy in

ministerial relationships, see Marie M. Fortune, *Responding to Clergy Misconduct: A Handbook* (Seattle: FaithTrust Institute, 2009), 28, 49-50; Karen Lebacqz and Ronald G. Barton, *Sex in the Parish*, 1st ed. (Louisville: Westminster John Knox, 1991), 113-31; Karen A. McClintock, *Preventing Sexual Abuse in Congregations: A Resource for Leaders* (Herndon: Alban Institute, 2004), 78-82.

8. See Marie M. Fortune, *Love Does No Harm: Sexual Ethics for the Rest of Us* (New York: Continuum, 1995), 83-4.

9. Karen Lebacqz and Ronald G. Barton caution that the burden of proof is on the pastor to demonstrate that the relationship is genuinely consensual and that the couple are meeting as equals and that the culturally reality of sexism renders a relationship between a male pastor and a female congregant unlikely to be free of power and coercion: *Sex in the Parish*, 1st ed. (Louisville: Westminster John Knox, 1991), 130.

8. Clery Sexual Abuse of Adults • *Pamela Cooper-White*

1. "Katya" and "Peg" are not their real names. Details of their stories have been altered to maintain confidentiality. Both stories are reprinted by permission.

2. For information on sexual abuse of children by clergy, see my book, *The Cry of Tamar*, on child sexual abuse. Sexual contact with minors is illegal in all 50 states. The largest and most active organization for survivors of childhood clergy sexual abuse, with a strong emphasis on abuse in the Roman Catholic Church, is SNAP (Survivors Network of those Abused by Priests), online at www.snapnetwork.org, accessed Sept. 7, 2011.

3. Marie M. Fortune, *Is Nothing Sacred? When Sex Invades the Pastor-Parishioner Relationship* (San Francisco: Harper and Row, 1989); see also Fortune and James N. Poling, *Sexual Abuse by Clergy: A Crisis for the Church* (Decatur: Journal of Pastoral Care Publications, 1994).

4. Peter Rutter, M.D., *Sex in the Forbidden Zone: When Men in Power Abuse Women's Trust* (Los Angeles: Jeremy Tarcher, 1989).

5. For an excellent review of related literature on therapist-client sexual contact, see Gary R. Schoener, "A Look at the Literature," in *Psychotherapists' Sexual Involvement with Clients: Intervention and Prevention* (Minneapolis: Walk-In Counseling Center, 1989), 11–50. Key prevalence studies include:

S. H. Kardener, M. Fuller, and I. Mensh, "A Survey of Physicians' Attitudes and Practices regarding Erotic and Nonerotic Contact with Clients," *American Journal of Psychiatry* 130 (1973), 1077–81; J. C. Holroyd and A. M. Brodsky, "Psychologists' Attitudes and Practices regarding Erotic and Nonerotic Physical Contact with Patients," *American Psychologist* 32 (1977), 843–49; Kenneth S.

Pope, H. Levinson, and L. Schover, "Sexual Intimacy in Psychology Training: Results and Implications of a National Survey," *American Psychologist* 34 (1979), 682–89; J. Bouhoutsos, J. Holroyd, H. Herman, B. Forer, and M. Greenberg, "Sexual Intimacy between Psychotherapists and Patients," *Professional Psychology: Research and Practice* 14 (1983), 185–96; J. Hamilton and H. DeRosis, *Report of the Women's Committee to the Washington, D.C., Psychiatric Society* (Washington, D.C.: Washington Psychiatric Society, 1985); Kenneth S. Pope, P. Keith-Spiegel, and B. G. Tabachnick, "Sexual Attraction to Clients: The Human Therapist and the (Sometimes) Inhuman Training System," *American Psychologist* 41 (1986), 147–58; N. Gartrell, J. Herman, S. Olarte, M. Feldstein, and R. Localio, "Psychiatrist-Patient Sexual Contact: Results of a National Survey, I: Prevalence," *American Journal of Psychiatry* 143 (1986), 1126–31; N. Gartrell et al. "Reporting Practices of Psychiatrists Who Knew of Sexual Misconduct by Colleagues," *American Journal of Ortho-Psychiatry* 57 (1987), 287–95; Kenneth S. Pope, B. G. Tabachnick, and P. Keith-Spiegel, "Ethics of Practice: The Beliefs and Behaviors of Psychologists as Therapists," *American Psychologist* 42 (1987), 993–1006; A. Bernsen, B.G. Tabachnick, and K.S. Pope,"National Survey of Social Workers' Sexual Attraction to their Clients: Results, Implications, and Comparison to Psychologists," *Ethics and Behavior* 4 (1994), 369-88.

6. A range of 12 to 20.7 percent can be extrapolated from a *Christianity Today* survey, reported in "How Common Is Pastoral Indiscretion?" *Leadership* (Winter 1988), 1. A doctoral study at Fuller Seminary shows fully 38.6 percent of respondents having had sexual contact with a parishioner. See Richard Allen Blackmon, "The Hazards of the Ministry" (unpublished Ph.D. dissertation, Fuller Seminary, 1984).

7. *Leadership,* 12.

8. Ibid., 13.

9. Stanley Grenz, "When the Pastoral Fails: Sexual Misconduct as a Betrayal of Trust," *Crux* 31/2 (1955), 23.

10. Blackmon, "The Hazards of the Ministry." Anthony Kuchan reports that 11.2 percent of all sexual contact reported to helping professionals were clergy, in "Survey of Incidence of Psychotherapists' Sexual Contact with Clients in Wisconsin," in Schoener et al., ed., *Psychotherapists' Sexual Involvement,* 60.

11. Bromley, David G., and Clinton H. Cress. 2000. "Narrative of Sexual Danger: A Comparative Perspective on the Emergence of the Clergy Sexual Violation Scandal," in *Bad pastors: Clergy Misconduct in Modern America,* ed. Anson Shupe, William A. Stacey, and Susan E. Darnell (New York: New York University Press), 39-68.

12. Perry Francis and James Stacks, "The Association between Spiritual Well-being and Clergy Sexual Misconduct," *Journal of Religion and Abuse* 5/1 (2003), 81.

13. Mark Chaves and Diana Garland, "The Prevalence of Clergy Sexual Advances towards Adults in Their Congregations," *Journal of the Scientific Study of Religion* 48/4 (2009), 820. Summarized online at Baylor University, "Clergy Sexual Misconduct Awareness and Prevention," www.baylor.edu/clergysexual-misconduct, accessed Aug. 10, 2011.

14. Baylor University, "Clergy Sexual Misconduct Awareness and Prevention,"

15. Ibid.

16. Ibid. Qualitative interviews in the Baylor study included participants from 17 different Christian and Jewish denominations.

17. Cooper-White, "The Use of the Self in Psychotherapy: A Comparative Study of Pastoral Counselors and Clinical Social Workers," *American Journal of Pastoral Counseling* 4/4 (2001), 5-35; also discussed in Cooper-White, *Shared Wisdom: Use of the Self in Pastoral Care and Counseling* (Minneapolis: Fortress Press, 2004), 155-80.

18. For an alternative, less absolute point of view, see Karen Lebacqz and Ronald G. Barton in "Sex, Power and Ministry: The Case of the Normal Neurotic," *Quarterly Review* 10/1 (1990); and *Sex in the Parish,* Westminster Press, 1991.

19. Pamela Cooper-White, "Soul-Stealing: Power Relations in Pastoral Sexual Abuse," *Christian Century,* February 20, 1991, 196–99.

20. See also Baylor University, "Clergy Sexual Misconduct Awareness and Prevention."

21. Bouhoutsos et al. ("Sexual Intimacy," 185–96), report that 92.4 percent of sexual contact was between male therapists and female clients.

22. See further explorations of this theme by Mary Pellauer, "Sex, Power and the Family of God," *Christianity and Crisis,* February 16, 1987.

23. It is largely to this complex reality that Karen Lebacqz and Ronald G. Barton speak in "Sex, Power and Ministry" and *Sex in the Parish.* They argue that it may be legitimate for single pastors to fall in love with single parishioners. Even in this less stringent treatment of the theme of pastor-parishioner dating, they also caution that a complex power dynamic must be taken into consideration. In *Sex in the Parish,* they further caution that certain public safeguards against secrecy and exploitation must be set up.

24. For several thoughtful essays on secondary victims, see Nancy Myer Hopkins and Mark Laaser, eds., *Restoring the Soul of a Church: Healing*

Congregations Wounded by Clergy Sexual Misconduct (Collegeville, MN: Alban Institute and Interfaith Sexual Trauma Institute, 1995), 55-197.

25. These states are Connecticut, Delaware, Iowa, Kansas, Minnesota, Mississippi, New Mexico, North Dakota, South Dakota, Utah, Wisconsin, and the District of Columbia, with legislation pending in Kansas, as discussed in Bradley Toben and Kris Helge, "Sexual Misconduct of Clergypersons with Congregants or Parishioners: Civil and Criminal Liabilities and Responsibilities," (2011), pp. 4, 28, online at http://www.baylor.edu/content/services/document.php/96096.pdf, and http://www.baylor.edu/clergysexualmisconduct/index.php?id=63297 under "Legislation Materials," accessed Aug. 10, 2011.

26. See also Marie M. Fortune, "Violating the Pastoral Relation" (review of Lebacqz and Barton), *Christianity and Crisis* 51/16–17, November 18, 1991, 367–68; Pamela Cooper-White, "Sex in the Parish" (review of Lebacqz and Barton), *Christian Century,* April 1, 1992, 344–45. Karen McClintock reviews the various real-life concerns related to single clergy dating in *Preventing Sexual Abuse in Congregations: A Resource for Leaders* (Herndon, VA: Alban Institute, 2004), 78-82. Referring to variations among denominational policies, she acknowledges some differences in official ethical guidelines, but remains firm in her statement that "sexualized contact between a pastor and a parishioner in the context of the ministerial role is *never consensual* because the clergy person has more power in the relationship." (78, emphasis added). Her model policy includes the statement, "Ministry professionals do not engage in sexual relationships with members or constituents of their congregations or other organizations they directly serve…" (138)

27. Lebacqz and Barton, *Sex in the Parish;* Karen Lebacqz, "Pastor-Parishioner Sexuality: An Ethical Analysis," *Explor* (Winter 1988); Lebacqz and Barton, "Sex, Power and Ministry," 36–48.

28. Ninety percent of victims reported harm in one study of therapist-patient sex (Bouhoutsos et al., "Sexual Intimacy," 185–96).

29. As Karen McClintock has written more recently, "as we get to know one another, we find that we are all vulnerable adults in search of safety…" in *Preventing Sexual Abuse in Congregations: A Resource for Leaders* (Herndon, VA: Alban Institute, 2004), 61.

30. Rutter, *Sex In the Forbidden Zone,* 182–84.

31. See Lebacqz and Barton's helpful chapter on "the Bishop's dilemma" in *Sex in the Parish;* Laaser and Hopkins, *Restoring the Soul of a Church.*

32. Marie M. Fortune, *Clergy Misconduct: Sexual Abuse in the Ministerial Relationship Workshop Manual* (Seattle: FaithTrust Institute, 1992), 20–21.

33. Schoener, *Psychotherapists' Involvement with Clients,* 402–4.

34. For this reason, clinical typologies are not designed to be used diagnostically, but for educational purposes. Clinical assessment is based on the prognosis for rehabilitation, by what means, and how it can be measurable and made accountable to future congregations.

35. Gary Schoener, personal communication; G. Lloyd Rediger, *Ministry and Sexuality: Cases, Counseling, and Care* (Minneapolis: Fortress Press, 1992), 24. One study showed 80 percent of offenders with more than one client (median=2, mean=2.6 clients). J. C. Holroyd and A. M. Brodsky, "Psychologists' attitudes and practices," 843–49. From a purely statistical point of view, if even half of offenders abuse at least two victims, then at least two-thirds of all victims will have been abused by a repeat offender. This has important implications for the importance of doing public investigations of single allegations, in order to allow other victims to come forward.

36. Similar theoretical models of multiple causation have been applied to child sexual abuse by David Finkelhor, in *Child Sexual Abuse: New Theory and Research* (New York: Free Press, 1984), 33–68; to sexual assault and battery of women by Diana Russell, *Sexual Exploitation: Rape, Child Sexual Abuse, and Sexual Harassment* (Beverly Hills: Sage, 1984); and to the causative role of pornography in rape by Diana Russell, *Against Pornography* (Berkeley, Calif.: Russell Publications, 1993), 118ff.

37. One recent exception is G. Lloyd Rediger, *Ministry and Sexuality.* Although Rediger's focus is on sexuality and not power and professional ethics per se, he does name abuse clearly and frames clergy sexual ethics in terms of professional responsibility.

38. For example, Don Basham, *Lead Us Not into Temptation: Confronting Immorality in Ministry* (Old Tappan, N.J.: Chosen Books, 1986); [n.a.], "The War Within Continues: An Update on a Christian Leader's Struggle with Lust," *Leadership* (Winter 1988), 24–33; Randy Alcorn, "Strategies to Keep from Falling," *Leadership* (Winter 1988), 42–47; Andre Bustanoby, "Counseling the Seductive Female: Can We Offer Help and Yet Remain Safe?" *Leadership* (Winter 1988), 48–54. The best of this genre is Charles Rassieur, *The Problem Clergymen Don't Talk About* (Philadelphia: Westminster, 1976). While the emphasis of the book is still on resisting seduction by women parishioners, Rassieur does appeal to professionalism and a standard of care. Power dynamics remain largely unexplored.

39. For example, Martin Shepard's widely read *The Love Treatment: Sexual Intimacy between Patients and Psychotherapists* (New York: Peter H. Wyden, 1971). For a review of these debates see Schoener, "A Look at the Literature," 13–24.

40. McClintock, *Preventing Sexual Abuse in Congregations*, 103-110.

41. Gary Schoener and Jeanette H. Milgrom, "Sexual Exploitation by Clergy and Pastoral Counselors," in Schoener et al., *Psychotherapists' Sexual Involvement*, 230–32; Gary L. Harbaugh and E. Rogers, "Pastoral Burnout: A View from the Seminary," *Journal of Pastoral Care* 38/2 (1984), 99–106; Mary Pellauer, "Sex, Power and the Family of God," *Christianity and Crisis*, February 16, 1987, 49.

42. H. N. Malony, "Clergy Stress: Not So Bad After All?" *Ministry* (May 1989), 8–9.

43. In my view, McClintock relies too heavily on this model in her otherwise very helpful resource *Preventing Sexual Abuse in Congregations*, 83-102. By shifting the focus from gender and power to sexual shame and addiction, this approach sidesteps the primary dynamic of abuse of power and sexual exploitation of parishioners. The pitfalls of sex addiction treatment will be discussed further below.

44. Cf. Florence Rush, *The Best Kept Secret* (New York: Prentice-Hall, 1980).

45. Conrad Weiser gives a table summarizing studies of mental health of clergy and seminarians in *Healers—Harmed and Harmful* (Minneapolis: Fortress Press, 1994), 5. Some have suggested that the ministry attracts a certain type of narcissistic and competitive male personality—Andre Bustanoby, "The Pastor and the Other Woman," *Christianity Today*, August 30, 1974, 7–10; J. Reid Meloy, "Narcissistic Psychopathology and the Clergy," *Pastoral Psychology* 35/1 (1986), 50–55. More recent studies have presented a mixed and contradictory picture, e.g., J. Patrick, "Assessment of Narcissistic Psychopathology in the Clergy," *Pastoral Psychology* 38/3 (1998), 173-80; Hessel J. Zondag's review of the literature in "Just Like Other People: Narcissism among Pastors," *Pastoral Psychology* 52/5 (2004), 423-37. Zondag's own research found that 90 percent of Dutch pastors in his survey ranked as one of four narcissistic types: "balanced" (relatively low on both overt and covert types of narcissism), "undisguised" (overt), "vulnerable" (covert) and "masking" (high on both overt and covert), with implications ranging from adaptive self-esteem to dangerous self-inflation and manipulation of others (433-35).

46. See Samuel L. Bradshaw, "Ministers in Trouble: A Study of 140 Cases Evaluated at the Menninger Foundation," *Journal of Pastoral Care* 31/4 (December 1977), 236.

47. For an excellent understanding of narcissistic wounding, see Alice Miller, *The Drama of the Gifted Child: The Search for the True Self* (New York: Basic Books, 1981); specific to clergy, see J. Reid Meloy, "Narcissistic Psychopathology and the Clergy"; Conrad Weiser, *Healers—Harmed and Harmful*, esp. 67–81.

48. For more on narcissistic clergy and the relationship of boundary violations and countertransference, see the case of "Terence" in Cooper-White, *Shared Wisdom*, 102-22.

49. Pellauer, "Sex, Power, and the Family of God," 49.

50. For example, Robert J. Stout, "Clergy Divorce Spills into the Aisle," *Christianity Today,* February 5, 1982; and the emphasis on the theme of temptation in several articles in *Leadership,* Winter 1988; Louis McBurney, "Seduced," *Leadership* (Fall 1998), 101-106

51. See Ann-Janine Morey, "Blaming the Woman for the Abusive Male Pastor," *The Christian Century,* October 5, 1988, 866–69.

52. Gary Schoener and Jeanette H. Milgrom, "False or Misleading Complaints," in Schoener et al., *Psychotherapists' Sexual Involvement,* 147–56.

53. As dramatized in the training video "Not in My Church" (Seattle: FaithTrust Institute, 1991).

54. Cf. T. Gutheil, "Borderline Personality Disorder, Boundary Violations, and Patient-Therapist Sex: Medicolegal Pitfalls," *American Journal of Psychiatry* 146 (1989), 597–602.

55. Karen McClintock gives helpful guidelines for how to say "no" firmly and respectfully if a parishioner expresses sexual interest, in *Preventing Sexual Abuse in Congregations,* 73-77.

56. For a discussion of liability from a pastor's point of view, see Richard R. Hammar, *Pastor, Church and Law, Vol. 1: Legal Issues for the Pastor* (Carol Stream IL: Your Church Resources/Christianity Today International, 2008), 308-339.

57. For more detailed guidelines for reporting pastoral sexual abuse, see the Center for Women and Religion, *A Clergy Abuse Survivor's Resource Packet,* 3d rev. ed., November 1993 (2400 Ridge Road, Berkeley, CA 94709).

58. For a more detailed discussion of counseling adult victims, see Cooper-White, "Sexual Exploitation and Other Boundary Violations in Pastoral Ministries," in *Clinical Handbook of Pastoral Counseling, Vol. 3,* ed. Robert J. Wicks, Richard D. Parsons and Donald Capps (Mahwah, NJ: Paulist Press, 2003), 352-55.

59. See Arthur Gross-Schaefer and Jan Singer, "Clergy Sexual Misconduct: A Call for a Faithful, Not a Fearful, Response," *Congregations: The Alban Journal* (May/June 1993), 13–14. Helpful articles on legal issues include T. E. Denham and M. L. Denham, "Avoiding Malpractice Suits in Pastoral Counseling," *Pastoral Psychology* 35/2 (1986), 83–93; Deborah M. House, "Clergy Sexual Misconduct: The Church's Legal Liabilities," *Circuit Rider* (September 1992), 8–9; Donald C. Clark, Jr., "Sexual Abuse in the Church: The Law Steps In," *Christian Century,* April 4, 1993, 396–98.

60. Draft work by the Sexual Ethics Task Force of the Episcopal Diocese
of California, Spring 1992. Barbara Blodgett frames this similarly in terms of
the need for a "culture of responsibility" that goes beyond regulations, background checks and "audits" *in Lives Entrusted: An Ethic of Trust for Ministry*
(Minneapolis: Fortress, 2008), 56-58. She points out that "safety rules and procedures are lilke background checks: they can lull a congregation into thinking
it has done 'enough.'" P. 67.

61. Nathaniel S. Lehrman, "The Normality of Sexual Feelings in Pastoral
Counseling," *Pastoral Psychology,* 49–52.

62. Charles Rassieur was already advocating this approach in 1976 in *The
Problem Clergymen Don't Talk About.* Note that, in the light of more recent learn-
ings about abuse, Rassieur's consideration of reporting sexual feelings to a counselee is almost always ill advised.

63. William E. Hulme, "Sexual Boundary Violations of Clergy," in *Sexual
Exploitation in Professional Relationships,* ed. Glen O. Gabbard (Washington,
D.C.: American Psychiatric Press, 1989), 189–90.

64. David J. Rolfe, "The Destructive Potential of Psychological Counseling
for Pastor and Parish," *Pastoral Psychology* 34/1 (1985), 61–68.

65. For example, Patrick Carnes, *Out of the Shadows: Understanding Sexual
Addiction* (Minneapolis: CompCare, 1983); Sex and Love Addicts Anonymous
(SLAA)—a 12 step group, online at http://www.slaafws.org/, accessed Nov. 5,
2011. For a critique of the SLAA model as ignoring the larger socio-political
context of gender and power, see Christine F. Saulnier, "Images of the twelve-
step model, and sex and love addiction in an alcohol intervention group for
Black women," *Journal of Drug Issues* 26/1 (2006), 95–124.

66. Rutter, *Sex in the Forbidden Zone;* Sissela Bok, "Lies Protecting Peers
and Colleagues," in *Lying: Moral Choice in Public and Private Life* (New York:
Vintage/Random House, 1979), 161–66.

67. Chilton Knudsen, "Understanding Congregational Dynamics," in Laaser
and Hopkins, *Restoring the Soul of a Church*, 75-100; in the same volume see also
Nancy Myer Hopkins, "Living through the Crisis," 201-230 and Mark Laaser,
"Long-term Healing," 232-249.

68. Knudsen, ibid., and "Trauma De-Briefing: A Congregational Model,"
Conciliation Quarterly 10 (1991), 12.

69. Peter Eisler, "Church Abuse Cases and Lawyers: An Uneasy Mix," *USA
Today*, May 9, 2011; see also Nancy Myer Hopkins, "Living through the Crisis,"
in Laaser and Hopkins, *Restoring the Soul of a Church*, 201.

70. For example, see the appendix in Fortune, *Is Nothing Sacred?* For churches
struggling to harmonize sexual ethics policies with canonical and constitutional

disciplinary requirements, pioneering work has also been done, for example, in the Episcopal Church dioceses of Minnesota, Chicago, Boston, Los Angeles, and California, and in a number of synods of the Evangelical Lutheran Church in America. A model in the Roman Catholic Church is being developed in the Archdiocese of Chicago.

71. Arthur Gross-Schaefer, Lee Feldman and Nicole Perkowitz, "A Time to Learn: A Comparison of Policies Dealing with Clergy Sexual Misconduct," *Pastoral Psychology* 60/2 (2011), 223-31.

72. See also FaithTrust Institute, *Responding to Clergy Misconduct* (Seattle, WA: FaithTrust Institute, 2009); Baylor University, "Strategies for Preventing CSM," online at http://www.baylor.edu/clergysexualmisconduct/indexphp?id=67411, accessed Aug. 10, 2011.

73. Blodgett, *Lives Entrusted,* 80-81.

74. For excellent training resources for denominations and congregations, contact the FaithTrust Institute, 1914 N. 34th St. #105, Seattle, WA 98103. In particular, I have found two training DVDs to be invaluable: "Not in My Church" and more recently, the interfaith DVD curriculum, "A Sacred Trust: Boundary Issues for Clergy and Spiritual Teachers" (2003). Information online at http://www.faithtrustinstitute.org/store/clergy-ethics/dvds, accessed Aug. 10, 2011. For a sample of model policies and denominational prevention and training resources, see also [Episcopal] Church Pension Group, "Preventing Sexual Misconduct," online at https://www.cpg.org/active-clergy/insurance/preventing-sexual-misconduct/overview/, accessed Aug. 15, 2011.

75. Resources are now available for congregational healing in the aftermath of clergy sexual abuse. See, e.g., Chilton Knudsen, "Trauma Debriefing: A Congregational Model," in *MCS Conciliation Quarterly* (Spring 1991), 12–13; Nancy Myer Hopkins, "Symbolic Church Fights: The Hidden Agenda When Clerical Trust Has Been Betrayed," *Congregations: The Alban Journal* (May/June 1993), 15–18; Hopkins and Laaser, *Restoring the Soul of a Church*; Cooper-White, "Sexual Exploitation and Other Boundary Violations in Pastoral Ministry," esp. 355-62.

76. Details of appropriate diagnosis and treatment of professional sexual misconduct are exhaustively presented in Gary Schoener, Jeanette Milgrom, John Gonsiorek, Ellen Luepker, and Ray Conroe, *Psychotherapists' Sexual Involvement with Clients: Intervention and Prevention* (Minneapolis: Walk-In Counseling Center, 2451 Chicago Ave. South, Minneapolis MN 55404), 1989.

77. Blodgett, *Lives Entrusted*, 81.

78. Christie Cozad Neuger, "Working to Prevent Clergy Sexual Misconduct," *Reflective Practice: Formation and Supervision for Ministry* 30 (2010), 166.

79. E.g., Linda Hansen Robison, "The Abuse of Power: A View of Sexual Misconduct in a Systemic Approach to Pastoral Care," *Pastoral Psychology* 52/5 (2004), 395-404; see also Candace Benyei, *Understanding Clergy Misconduct in Religious Systems* (New York: Haworth Pastoral Press, 1998); McClintock, *Preventing Sexual Abuse in Congregations*, 51-68; Nancy Biale, "Creating Safer Congregations," in Beth Ann Gaede, ed., *When a Congregation Is Betrayed* (Herndon, VA: Alban Institute, 2005),147-55; and especially with regard to the aftermath of clergy misconduct, see also Laaser and Hopkins, *Restoring the Soul of a Church.*

80. Ibid., 167.

19. Self-Questioning from the Caribbean • *Nicqui Ashwood*

1. It is important to note that several Levitical laws are very specific in their reference to women as harlots and immoral creatures, however, the Torah is also very clear on the persons with whom one should not seek sexual relations.

2. Several of the Solomonic proverbs present women as harlots and adulteresses, suggesting that we are the ones who incite men's passions and cause them to revert to a more base nature. In Jamaica and several other spaces, it is a running "joke"/debate that the fruit mentioned in the story of the Fall is none other than coitus. If this is actually internalized, one sees yet again, where a woman is denied the role of victim, for she is charged with seducing the man..

3. See, for example, Prov. 23:7-8; Prov 31:10ff ; Luke 7:37, 39; John 4:6-7.

30. Criminalizing Misconduct • *Darryl W. Stephens*

1. See http://www.umc-gbcs.org/site/apps/nlnet/content.aspx?c=frLJK2PKL qFandb=6327129andct=8799947.

2. National Organization for Women: http://www.now.org/organization/conference/resolutions/2009.html#call and http://www.now.org/issues/violence/clergyabuse_statement.html and http://www.now.org/issues/violence/clergyabuse_unsafe.html.

3. "Sexual Misconduct within Ministerial Relationships," *The Book of Resolutions of the United Methodist Church 2008* (Nashville: UM Publishing House, 2008), 133-39

4. On the lack of meaningful consent in ministerial relationships, see Marie M. Fortune, *Responding to Clergy Misconduct: A Handbook*(Seattle: FaithTrust Institute, 2009), 28, 49-50; Karen Lebacqz and Ronald G. Barton, *Sex in the Parish*, 1st ed.(Louisville, Ky.: Westminster/J. Knox Press, 1991), 113-131; Karen A. McClintock, *Preventing Sexual Abuse in Congregations: A Resource for Leaders* (Herndon, Va.: Alban Institute, 2004), 78-82.

5. Diana Garland, "The Prevalence of Clergy Sexual Misconduct with Adults: A Research Study Executive Summary " (2009). http://www.baylor.edu/clergy-sexualmisconduct/index.php?id=67406 (accessed 16 July 2010). Also in this volume, as Chapter 3.

6. I am indebted to researchers at Baylor University for data and legal strategy presented in this section. Toben, Bradley J.B., and Kris Helge, "Sexual Misconduct of Clergypersons with Congregants or Parishioners—Civil and Criminal Liabilities and Responsibilities," http://www.baylor.edu/content/services/document.php/96096.pdf,.

31. Fundamental Reform • *Terry O'Neill*

1. For more information, see: *NOW Fact Sheet and Action Guide: Sexual Abuse of Women by Clergy;* "Unsafe in Any Denomination—Women and Clergy Sexual Abuse" by Nancy Quirk, Virginia NOW Activist; "Girls as Victims—The Emerging Story of Clergy Sex Abuse" by Jan Erickson, Director of Programs, NOW Foundation.

Additional Resources

Books on Clergy Sexual Abuse of Women

Angela Bonavoglia, *Good Catholic Girls: How Women are Leading the Fight to Change the Church.* San Francisco: HarperOne, 2005. See esp. ch. 5.

Pamela Cooper-White, *The Cry of Tamar: Violence against Women and the Church's Response.* 2d. ed. Minneapolis: Fortress Press, 2012.

Kathryn A. Flynn, *The Sexual Abuse of Women by Members of the Clergy.* McFarland & Co., 2003

Marie M. Fortune, *Is Nothing Sacred? When Sex Invades the Pastoral Relationship.* San Francisco: HarperSanFrancisco, 1992.

Beth A. Gaede, editor, *When a Congregation Is Betrayed: Responding to Clergy Misconduct.* Bathesda, Md.: Alban Institute, 2005.

Dee Ann Miller, *How Little We Knew: Collusion and Confusion with Sexual Misconduct.* Prescott Press, 1993.

Marilyn R Peterson, *At Personal Risk: Boundary Violations in Professional-Client Relationships.* New York: Norton, 1992.

Nancy W. Poling and Marie M. Fortune, *Victim to Survivor: Women Recovering from Clergy Sexual Abuse.* Portland, Ore.: Wipf & Stock, 1999.

Peter Rutter, M.D., *Sex in the Forbidden Zone: When... Therapists, Doctors, Clergy, Teachers and Other Men in Power Betray Women's Trust.* Aquarian Press, 1995.

Beth Van Dyke, *What About Her? A True Story of Clergy Abuse Survival.* Winepress Publishing, 1997.

Carolyn Waterstradt, *Fighting the Good Fight: Healing and Advocacy after Clergy Sexual Assault.* Splattered Ink Press, 2012.

H.J Wisocki and C.J. Scajnecki, *Innocence Betrayed: A Dad's Story of Clergy Misconduct.* PublishAmerica, 2007.

Organizations

World Health Organization (WHO)
WHO's Sexual Violence Research Initiative is a consortium, established by WHO and the Global Forum for Health Research, that aims to promote research on sexual violence and generate empirical data that ensures sexual violence is recognized as a priority public health problem.
http://www.who.int/reproductivehealth/topics/violence/sexual_

Faith Trust Institute
A multifaith, multicultural training and education organization founded in 1977 by the Rev. Dr. Marie M. Fortune, with global reach, working to end sexual and domestic violence. The institute provides communities and advocates with the tools and knowledge they need to address the religious and cultural issues related to clergy sexual abuse.
www.faithtrustinstitute.org

Survivors Network of Those Abused by Priests (SNAP)
A self-help group that supports people who have been victimized by clergy and helps them pick up the pieces of their lives, heal and move forward. SNAP also cooperates with news media and provides reliable information when possible, as a way to help recovery and prevent future abuse.
www.survivorsnetwork.org

Tamar's Voice
A religious non-profit organization that ministers to those who have been sexually abused by members of the clergy. Executive Director Jan Tuin is a survivor and therefore understands and empathizes with those who have experienced the devastation of clergy sexual abuse as well as the hope of healing.
www.tamarsvoice.org/about

Helpful Websites

Sharon's Rose
The purpose of this website is to give voice to survivors of clergy sexual abuse by providing resources, information, encouragement and hope and to provide awareness and understanding about clergy sexual abuse.
http://sharonsrose.org/

Take Courage

The site by Dee Ann Miller, 'stands as a source of enlightenment, dispelling the darkness so often cruelly created when victims or advocates dare to speak truth about sexual and domestic violence to people of faith and/or power. It is unique because it primarily offers insights into collusion, rather than the primary abuses of perpetrators.

http://www.takecourage.org

Acknowledgments

The editor acknowledges the written contributions, funding, reprint permissions, and personal encouragement that have supported this project.

First, this book could not have been published without generous support from many people.

I am deeply grateful to the survivors who have had the courage to talk of their experiences. Thank you to all the advocates, project workers, supporters, academics and journalists who have contributed their knowledge and wisdom. To the sponsoring organizations, the World Student Christian Federation and the World Council of Churches's programme of Women in Church and Society readers owe a deep debt. Special thanks to Dr. Fulata Lusungu Moyo, Christine Housel, Sofie Eriksen, Sunita Suna, Nectarinia Montes, Rey Asis, David Masters, Luciano Kovacs, Jooa Vourinen and Rachel Weber for their invaluable support and to the Denmark Student Christian Movement for raising the necessary funding.

Second, I am humbled and encouraged by the willingness of pioneers and experts in the field to contribute to this effort, including former US President Jimmy Carter, Rev. Dr. Marie Fortune, Rev. Dr. Pamela Cooper-White, Dr. Gary Schoener, Prof. Diana Garland, A. W. Richard Sipe, Prof. Samuel Gotay, Dr. Margaret Kennedy, Dee Miller, Dr. Darryl Stephens and Joan Winship.

Third, I offer my gratitude to Dr. Gary Schoener, my husband Dr. Andrew Batchelor, Prof. Carolyn Taylor, Garry Prior, and Amanda Gearing for inspiration, advice, practical assistance and editing skills.

Lastly, I gratefully acknowledge the generous help of authors, publishers, and church bodies for their permission to reprint specific contributions in this work, to wit:

Foreword: To the Carter Center, Atlanta, for permission to reprint President Jimmy Carter's presentation to the World Parliament of Religions.

Chapter 1: Gary Schoener: Previous versions of this article were presented at the Interfaith Conference on Clergy Sexual Misconduct: Helping Survivors and

Communities to Heal, 20 January 2005; Archdiocese of St. Paul & Minneapolis, St. Catherine University, University of St. Thomas.

Chapter 2: Marie M. Fortune. This article was previously printed in *Transforming a Rape Culture (Revised Edition),* Buchwald, Fletcher, Roth Eds. (Milkweed Editions, 2005). We acknowledge the author and the publisher Milkweed Editions for permission to reprint this article.

Chapter 3: Diana R. Garland. Used with permission. Visit the study web site at http://www.baylor.edu/clergysexualmisconduct/. Co-investigators of this study are Diana R. Garland, LCSW, Ph.D., Dean and Professor of Social Work, Baylor University; and Mark Chaves, Ph.D., Professor of Sociology, Religion, and Divinity, Duke University.

Chapter 4: Margaret Kennedy. This article is an excerpt from the introductory chapter of the author's thesis submitted to London Metropolitan University for the degree of Doctor of Philosophy in April 2009.

Chapter 5: Dee Ann Miller. We acknowledge Dee Ann Miller for permission to reprint this article, which appears on her website, www.takecourage.org. She is also the author of *How Little We Knew: Collusion and Confusion with Sexual Misconduct* and *The Truth about Malarkey.*

Chapter 6: Darryl W. Stephens. This is a revision of an article previously published the author's *Living the Sacred Trust: Clergy Sexual Ethics* (Nashville: General Board of Higher Education and Ministry, 2010).

Chapter 7: A. W. Richard Sipe. A previous version of this article was presented by the author Richard Sipe as a lecture at Survivor Network of Those Abused by Priest (SNAP) National Conference, Jersey City, New Jersey July 21-23, 2006.

Chapter 8: Pamela Cooper-White. Reprinted with permission of the author and Fortress Press from *Cry of Tamar: Violence against Women and the Church's Response.* 2d ed. (Minneaopolis: Fortress Press, 2012).

Chapter 12: Amanda Gearing. This article was published in WSCF Europe's publication *Mozaik 26, Stop Being Silent,* 2010, and is printed with permission.

Chapter 13: Rex Host. With permission of the author.

Chapter 14: Ann Kennedy. By permission of the author.

Chapter 15: Valli Batchelor. Used with permission. A previous version of this article appears on the "Ecumenical Women at the UN" website; used with permission.

Chapter 16: Victor Kaonga. Used with permission.

Chapter 17: Samantha Nelson. Used with permission.

Chapter 18: Lori McPherson. Used with permission.

Chapter 19: Nicqui Ashwood. Used with permission.

Chapter 20: Esther Lubunga Kenge. Used with permission.

Chapter 21: Janejinda Pawadee. A previous version of this article as published in *CCA (Council of Churches Asia) News,* December 2007.

Chapter 22: Kenneth Dobson. Used with permission.

Chapter 23: Susan Jamison. Reprinted with permission from *The Flyer Online,* vol. 42/3 (March 2011), the General Commission on the Status and Role of Women, the United Methodist Church.

Chapter 24: Sally Dolch. Used with permission.

Chapter 25: David Masters. Used with permission.

Chapter 26: Luciano Kovacs. Used with permission.

Chapter 27: Marie M. Fortune. This chapter previously appeared as a blog entry from the author on August 22, 2008, and is used with permission of the author and the FaithTrust Institute.

Chapter 28: Martin Weber. This chapter was previously published in WSCF's *Mozaik 26: Stop Being Silent,* 2010, adapted from previous publication on the website of The Hope of Survivors. We are grateful to the author, to The Hope of Survivors, and to WSCF—Europe for permission to reprint.

Chapter 29: Darryl W. Stephens. Revised with permission from the author's *Living the Sacred Trust: Clergy Sexual Ethics* (Nashville: General Board of Higher Education and Minsitry, 2010).

Chapter 30: Terry O'Neill. Reprinted with permission from the National Organization for Women USA website, www.now.org.

Chapter 31: Cléo Fatoorehchi. Inter Press Service (IPS) United Nations is acknowledged for its support and permission to print this article, previously published by IPS on February 27, 2011.

Chapter 32: M. Garlinda Burton. Reprinted with permission from United Methodist News Service.

Chapter 33: Gary R. Schoener. Reprinted by permission of the author and the Walk-In Center, Minneapolis.